CONSCIENCE

AND ACTION

SOCIAL STATEMENTS OF THE AMERICAN LUTHERAN CHURCH

EDITED BY CARL F REUSS 1961-1970

AUGSBURG PUBLISHING HOUSE
MINNEAPOLIS   MINNESOTA

CONSCIENCE AND ACTION

Library of Congress Catalog Card No. 75-135223

International Standard Book No. 0-8066-1106-5

Manufactured in the United States of America

CONSCIENCE
AND

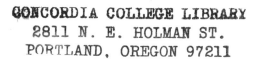

Contents

I

Conscience and Action

Lutheran churches are alleged to have little or no interest in social questions. For The American Lutheran Church, at least, that allegation is false. From the initial meeting of its new Church Council in 1961, down to the present, this church body has evidenced a lively and growing interest in social questions. Its conscience has been pricked by the evils, injustices, and inequities it sees in society. It has sought courses of action appropriate both for itself as a corporate body and for its members active in the structures of society.

A RECORD OF CONCERN

This volume records that pricking of conscience and that quest for action over the decade 1961-1970. It compiles the formal statements and resolutions relating to social issues as these were acted upon either by the broadly-representative General Convention or by the 45-member Church Council, which bears legislative authority in the interim between the biennial conventions.* It is a record of the effort to fulfill one of the subpurposes to which The American Lutheran Church constitutionally is committed:

Study the problems of contemporary life and society in the light of the Word of God, in order to make its contribution toward solving these problems.

---

* Appreciation is expressed to Dr. Byron L. Schmid, formerly assistant director of the Commission on Research and Social Action, for the preliminary research and analysis on which this volume is based.

How one church body has sought to deal with social questions in a manner consistent with its understanding of its mission and its resources will interest not only its own members but also many persons in a far wider circle. Particularly may persons of other religious persuasions and persons moved solely by humanitarian considerations take exception to the stance of The American Lutheran Church. This is to be expected. Yet, such persons also may find much to agree with in the analyses and conclusions recorded in this volume. After all, The American Lutheran Church shares much in common with other Christians. Moreover, in its appeals to truth, justice, equity, and reason it appeals to essentially human values shared with all persons of good will. Thus it offers grounds for cooperation in humanitarian endeavors.

Several strands weave fairly consistently through the ALC actions. One emphasizes the pastoral role of the church, especially its function of teaching its members to seek out and to do what a faith active in love requires of them. A second is the conviction that the members sustain, stimulate, and support one another in the Christian fellowship of witness and service. A third takes seriously the idea of vocation, by which the called Christian moves in all the relations of life as a light and salt of Christian influence. A fourth holds that there is a higher law to which all authority figures must yield. Thus neither the state nor any other temporal authority may be given unchecked power. A fifth is that comment and counsel from the church to its members must evidence biblical moorings.

SOME CENTRAL BIBLICAL CONCEPTS

This latter quest for biblical moorings reflects itself in a number of areas. First, and centrally, in their Godward orientation The ALC statements generally recognize:

—God's creative and sustaining providence over all of his creation and all of his creatures, regardless of their relationship to Jesus Christ, divine Lord and Savior;

—The redemptive activity of God in Jesus Christ, offering pardon and salvation to all who accept his invitation, regardless of their age, sex, nationality, social status, or any other personal merits or demerits they feel they may have;

—The sanctifying power by which God's spirit works faith in the promises of God and readiness to serve neighbor as self; and that

—God's will for man is only good, positive, and gracious, though he permits man in man's exercise of free will to bring evils and problems onto himself and onto his life in society.

Relating to man and his nature The ALC statements generally reflect such biblically derived views as the following:

—Man is a social creature, fashioned in God's image. Man must live in fellowship with his neighbors and in community, under God, in order to realize his true humanity.

—Man is a sinful creature, rebelling against his Creator, doing what he should not do, failing to do what he should do, fouling his lines and relationships.

—Man is justified before God by his faith. Man justified by faith, with sins forgiven, is restored to fellowship with God and freed for self-giving service. When he is restored in his relationship to God, man has a liberated reorientation of views on himself, neighbor, nature, and society.

—The justified and forgiven man, though still a sinner, inescapably must have his faith issue in deeds of love and service as he takes his place responsibly in the structures of society.

Implicit in the various statements are undergirding assumptions about the structures and functioning of secular society. Among them are such as the following:

—All of this earth and all of its contents are the Lord's but God has entrusted these to man's stewardship and dominion. Man is expected to use these in responsible, God-pleasing, neighbor-serving ways, which at the same time are self-satisfying, self-fulfilling, and nonexploitive.

—Man's life in community is ordered and influenced by such basic institutions as marriage and the family, the economic order, the state and political processes, and religion and its structures. These socially essential institutions are designed by God to regulate, channel, and control the expression of man's basic drives and aspirations.

—God's commandments decreeing the honoring of the sacred and divine, and the preservation of the healthy tension between the person and the community, should be incorporated into the practical functioning of all social structures.

—When conditions in society hurt or harm persons, either singly or in their interrelationships, men must take effective measures both to care for the victims and also to correct the conditions which cause the distress.

A fourth area in which major assumptions can be identified relates to the church as a social institution. The statements of The ALC generally reflect such views as the following:

—The church relies on the power not of the sword but of the spirit. It works through the means of grace, whose promises are accepted in faith and whose power changes the hearts and lives of people.

—The central tasks of the church are to confront men with the claims of Jesus Christ, to make disciples of those who accept these claims, and to teach these persons the fullness of the demands of discipleship as the Lord taught them.

—The preoccupation and competence of the church are with spiritual matters as these pertain to man's eternal life and destiny. The church helps men to see and to use earthly things in the perspective of God's eternal purposes and his universal kingdom.

—Though the church is a corporate body, it is also the people of God at work in the world. These people of God participating as light and salt in the structures of society are committed to fill their various offices in society to the glory of God and in service to the neighbor.

OBSERVATIONS ON THE PROCESSES

Statements included in this compilation are of four major types. First are those originating with the Church Council. These typically are prepared at the Church Council meeting by an ad hoc committee of its own members and approved in Council plenary. A second category includes resolutions introduced by delegates to the General Convention, processed through the Convention Committee, and approved in Convention plenary. A third type includes statements made at the Convention sessions which were so favorably received that the Convention took formal action to give them broader standing.

The fourth category is the most voluminous. It includes statements initially prepared by the Commission on Research and Social Action. Typically these were widely circulated in preliminary form throughout the church to stimulate thinking and to promote discussion on the issue. Responses were sought and received from study groups in congregations, from district committees on research and social action, and from selected resource persons. In light of such responses the Commission would receive the draft before submitting it for Church Council review and General Convention action. The statement approved by the Convention might well have been the sixth to ninth draft, the preparation process extending over two to four years and involving hundreds, even thousands, of persons in the task of scrutiny, criticism, and correction. Indeed, many a preliminary draft never survived the process. Convention statements originating with the Commission on Research and Social Action normally are the culmination of an extended study process.

USEFULNESS OF THE STATEMENTS

Statements adopted by the Church Council or General Convention are binding on The American Lutheran Church only to the extent that they establish corporate policy for the church body and its respective organizational units. Statements of judgment and conviction or of comment and counsel have no binding character. They must gain assent and support by the inherent merits of the position and the weight of what is said. It is expected, nevertheless, that the actions taken by the Church Council or the General Convention will be accorded respect and serious consideration even by those who disagree with the action.

Most statements originating with the Commission on Research and Social Action attempt to define problems, offer a careful social analysis of causes, and consider probable consequences of proposed action or inaction. They fill a problem-orienting function. Others seek to articulate broad social goals, pointing in the direction of needed social change and the redevelopment of public policy. A third approach appeals to the sense of moral obligation to participate in the struggle against injustice and for civic betterment, relating the Christian commitment to political and social involvement. Throughout is the effort to provide accurate analyses as a prerequisite for moving an informed church, quickened in its conscience, into appropriate action for an effective attack on the social problems of its age.

II

The Church in Society

A. ITS SOCIAL INVOLVEMENT
Our Approach to Social Involvement

In origin, this statement began with "A Hard Look at Our Task" as reported by the Commission on Research and Social Action to the 1962 General Convention. The 1966 Convention commended "to the earnest study and discussion of pastors and of congregations" a statement on "The Church's Role in Society." In light of responses received, the Commission prepared "Our Approach to Social Involvement," which the 1968 Convention resolved should "be commended to the congregations of The American Lutheran Church for their use."

Church involvement in social action currently is a controversial question. Some see it as the only hope for a living and relevant church. Others see it as a force destructive of the church's prime mission. Against this background the Commission on Research and Social Action offers views it believes should be normative for The American Lutheran Church.

Our Confessional Stance

Consistent with its confessional stance, The American Lutheran Church accepts the doctrinal positions stated in the unaltered Augsburg Confession. Therein it finds wise and balanced counsel for its social action involvement. In the personal realm the Augsburg Confession steers between ethical activism and ethical quietism. In the social realm it affirms the secular and rejects ecclesiastical dominance over the secular.

14

On the personal level, as Article IV makes plain, no man can win his way into God's favor by his good works. Not even the most self-sacrificing social involvement can earn him salvation. Man becomes righteous before God solely by grace, for Christ's sake, through faith. However, the believer cannot relax in insulated indifference to human needs and social injustice. For, his faith is bound to produce good fruits, as Article VI affirms. Faith is moving, active, obedient. Faith heeds God's command to do, for his sake, the good works which serve neighbor and community. Social involvement is an inescapable fruit of a person's living faith in Jesus Christ.

On the social level Article XVI affirms the validity of the secular structures, including government, as part of God's created and sustaining order. It expects Christians to permeate every structure of society, therein faithfully to do those good works which advance truth, justice, mercy, peace, freedom, opportunity, responsibility, and the other qualities of civic righteousness. Article XXVIII denies to the church any claims to exercise power and authority over the temporal realm. It sharply distinguishes the powers and functions of both church and state, each under God, and insists that each be free to fulfill its own divine mandate without hindrance from the other.

Power and Resources of the Church

The church relies on the power of the gospel and the leading of the Spirit to draw men to saving faith in the mighty acts and the lifegiving promises of the triune God. It seeks through the same Spirit to make faithful and God-revering disciples, to teach these disciples all that the Lord commands them, to unite these disciples in living bonds of fellowship with the Lord and with one another, to equip these disciples for ministry in accord with their individual abilities, and to empower and embolden these same disciples for their witness and service as light, leaven, and salt in the structures of secular society.

This approach recognizes that the church is both an organized corporate body and the people of God at work in his world. The corporate church equips its members for mission. It assists, strengthens, and upholds them in their ministry. But, the corporate church neither takes over their mission nor substitutes for them in their ministry. The corporate church best involves itself in the issues of society when in its teaching, pastoral, and fellowship roles it prepares its members to take their places warmly, wisely, and responsibly in their various offices in secular society.

Avenues for Supportive Involvement

Toward this end, and consistent with its faith and its resources, the corporate church at its several levels of organization wisely structures itself to:

a. Analyze the issues causing tension and the values in conflict in the world, enlisting its keenest minds from among involved laity and discerning pastors to cut through to the heart of the issue, exposing the good and the evil, the sinful and the wholesome, that are in contention;

b. Evaluate the effects of current social trends upon persons individually, upon persons in their relationships with one another, and upon the ability of the various institutions and structures of society effectively to fulfill their special functions within the community;

c. Seek to discern and to communicate the meaning of the gospel for the rapidly changing human situation, taking care not to wrench Scripture out of context to make it support man's prejudices;

d. Clarify the goals and objectives for man and community toward which social planning should move, as well as the values and criteria by which men can judge the wisdom and wholesomeness of measures for civic righteousness;

e. Teach its members to act with knowledge, conviction, honor, and wisdom in their various civic offices, as Christians striving to accomplish God's purposes for justice, mercy, opportunity, peace, truth, freedom, and responsible relationships one with another in the family of mankind;

f. Strengthen, uphold, fortify, and renew these members in their ministry in society, communicating its willingness to serve as pastor, guide, counselor, brother, or sister, in working through with them the decisions they must reach as they faithfully seek to be Christ's disciples in the structures of society;

g. Resist any and every effort which would make the church captive of a particular class, political, economic, racial, national, or ideological interest, keeping itself free to proclaim that counsel and bear that witness which it believes its Lord expects of his church.

Avenues for Corporate, Involvement

Times and circumstances may cause the corporate church at its several levels to decide that faithfulness to Jesus Christ requires corporate involvement in specific social issues or problem situations. Again consistent with its faith, its mission, and its resources the church at any of its levels of organization may decide through duly constituted processes to:

a. Express its convictions in a resolution or statement adopted by a delegated assembly;

b. Deploy funds and manpower in pursuit of goals it deems essential to faithful discipleship;

c. Encourage its personnel in positions of trust and leadership to speak and to act as Spirit-enlightened wisdom guides them;

d. Establish and maintain institutions and agencies for dealing in reconciling and healing ways with issues or situations the church defines as critical;

e. Effect corporate relationships with other religious or civic organizations committed to achieving objectives the church regards as basic to effective civic righteousness.

The corporate church should rely upon its knowledgeable and articulate members for shaping ecclesiastical policies and positions on sensitive issues. Whatever the corporate church decides to do, however, must be consistent with its recognition of the organizational pluralism and proper functions of the several institutions of society, its disavowal of any claims to exercise control over the nonreligious institutions, and its acceptance of its own unique role as the avenue for God's mediating and reconciling means of grace.

Time for a Telling Witness

The times compel the corporate church to bestir itself about issues of injustice, exploitation, oppression, indifference, and insensitivity to others, hopelessness, denial of opportunity, and the abundant evidences of man's inhumanity to brother man. At its every level of organization the church needs to evidence its genuine interest in and its honest concern for all men, without regard for their wealth, prestige, social standing, race, political belief, or nationality. Its confession of faith begins with its recognition of God's hand and his will that the created universe serve his purposes. But, unlike any other institution in society, the church can proclaim the message of redemption and release and can point to the source of power for the changed hearts and changed lives so basic to better communities. As the church and its people pray and work for daily bread for all people, they recall that this request for temporal necessities comes between the petition that God's will be done and the petition that our trespasses be forgiven.

Uniquely the church can bring man's issues and relationships into a clearer perspective. It can bring a vision of the changeless and the counsel of the ages to bear upon the ever-new examples of the ages-old themes of man's struggle to find his own identity, to exercise dominion over the earth, to regulate his relationships with his fellows, and to seek what his God would have him do. The church must speak to the issues of the times. Yet, as the church deals with contemporary issues it does so in the knowledge of the presence of the living God before whom all men stand and to whom all men are accountable.

Sent into the World

The 1970 Convention adopted the following statement as "a word of comment and counsel to the members of the ALC." It was submitted by the Commission on Research and Social Action and endorsed by the General Convention Committee.

The General Convention Committee concurs with the Commission on Research and Social Action in its comment and concern as well as its challenge to commitment in the statement "Sent into the World."

We acknowledge that a careful delineation of the problems and a study of their complexities sharpens the sense of Christian responsibility. We also acknowledge the freedom and hope of the gospel which enables the people of God to demonstrate their faith in word and deed, and therefore commend this statement of the Commission to the church.

The Fifth General Convention of The American Lutheran Church takes to heart its theme, "Sent into the World." It is a call to plan and to do, to talk and to act upon its implications.

As we look at the world of which we are a part and into which we are sent, our feelings are mixed. We see much that is good, wholesome, and positive. We see many evidences of people working with, helping, and befriending one another. We see how useful, effective, and adaptable are many of the agencies and institutions of our society. We see many constructive changes in the attitudes, expectations, and actions of people. We thank God for the many blessings we enjoy as a people, a nation, and a church.

Yet our hearts also are heavy. We see tensions, conflicts, and problems that reach into every area of life. We feel some of the same anguish of spirit which caused the Savior to weep over the city of Jerusalem. What sensitive soul can help but feel anguish over certain trends, currents, and movements in our nation? What person, knowing that he is sent into the world can be silent and do nothing when people are hurt or suffer, when anarchy threatens, when people perish for lack of vision, when men make their own

gods and worship that which they have created? In the conviction
that recognition of problems gives opportunity for correction, we
single out a number of negative elements in American life. They
deserve attention and appropriate action by each of the levels of
organization of The American Lutheran Church, beginning with the
members of our congregations.

The Wide Range of Our Concerns

In the lives of many persons we note the growing reliance on
drugs in all strata of society, the greed which preys on selfish desires and sinful pride, the abuse of sexuality, and the massive
alienation which isolates so many persons from social participation
and social responsibility.

In American family life we note the prevalence of divorce and
desertion, the plight of the lonely, the elderly, and the handicapped,
and the unfulfilled struggles to identify the rights and the roles of
men, women, and youth in family and community.

In our communities we note the arson, bombings, murders, and
other violence, the resistance to authority, the growing use of repressive laws and policies, the gap between well-intended legislation and its effective implementation, the decaying inner cities and
the dying rural communities, and the unfulfilled drive for recognition and self-determination by racial and ethnic groups in our
midst.

In the economic sphere we note the tragedy of poverty and hunger
at home and abroad, the continuing inflation, rising unemployment,
the helplessness of people who lack effective political or economic
power, and the increasing pollution and deterioration of our natural
environment.

In our national life we note not merely continuing but indeed
hardening racism and racial tensions, manifest injustices and double
standards of justice, a broken confidence in either the willingness
or the ability of our social institutions to meet the needs of people,
the difficulties of dealing with dissent and disruption, and the difficulties our governments have in using their powers either effectively or appropriately.

On the international scene we note the continuing scourge of
war, whether declared or undeclared, whether hot or cold, the arms
race and the related reliance upon military might to settle disputes
between nations, the expanding influence of authoritarian ideologies
and regimes of the left and the right, the imbalances of power and

wealth among the nations, and the lagging enthusiasm for working with the younger nations of the world to help assure their viability, development, and vitality.

In our life within the church we note dissension concerning the source and the nature of its authority, concerning the role of the church in society, concerning the usefulness of organization and structures, as well as problems of trust and understanding between clergy and laity.

Everywhere we see the fruits of sin, man's rebellion against God, man's dehumanizing of brother man, man's estrangement from himself, man's exploitation of his environment. Yet men yearn for freedom, for peace, for justice, for the right to have a say in the decisions that affect their own destinies. Man's urgent need at this hour of history is his need to find his true humanity, grounded in a right relationship with God. For such a time as this we of the church are sent into the world. Our mission is that expressed in the gospel.

The Foundation of Our Concern

The gospel of Jesus Christ does not call his church from the world, but sends his church into the world. The conflicts and tensions of the world challenge the church to become its true self, the people of God sent into the world to speak and to live within the activity of God. God sent Jesus Christ into the world to speak and demonstrate the word of grace and reconciliation to the world's essential despair. Sending the church into the world is a part of God's ongoing movement in the world. The church is a sign to the world that God seeks to redeem and to help the world with its tensions and conflicts.

The world always lives in the tension of God's judgment and grace. Either to pronounce final judgment on the world and turn away from its predicament, or to see the world as redeeming itself through its own efforts is to misunderstand God's relation to the world. The church, as sent into the world, embraces the tension of judgment which condemns and grace which gives freedom.

The life of the church, shaped by the gospel, witnesses to God's love and God's reconciling action in the world. Nothing in the world is neutral or irrelevant to the gospel. The gospel does not abandon some dimensions of life and speak to others. It addresses the whole world of relationships: personal, family, community, economic, national, and international. The gospel addresses the whole creation and invites the whole creation into a new community with God. This is the gospel with which the church is sent into the world.

The Concern for Our Mission

This Fifth General Convention of The American Lutheran Church calls the whole of The American Lutheran Church to searching self-examination. How do our deeds square with our words? When the world looks at us and our activities, what does it see? Have we, too, undergone an erosion of honesty and credibility so that we are no longer the light that guides or the salt that heals? What do we define as our mission? How serious are we about that which we see as our mission? What time and attention do we give to study of the Scriptures, seeking God's direction and leadership? Where shall we apply the resources and energies God has given us? What do we see when we view ourselves in the mirror of Matthew 23, our Lord's jarring words to the religious establishment of that era?

It is not easy to accept the responsibility of being sent. In our human nature we prefer to send, not to be sent. We prefer to give orders, not to be under orders. We prefer to be principals, not agents. Yet in such a secondary role the church finds its primary mission. It is sent into the world by Jesus Christ. It is to the whole of his task that the church is committed. Jesus Christ came into the world because God loves the world, with all its tensions, conflicts, problems, and sin. He offers salvation, reconciliation, and a more abundant life to whomsoever will accept them. God's purpose is not to condemn but to save the world through faith in his only Son (John 3:17, 18). Faithful to this vision we indeed are ready to be sent into the world.

Decision in a Time of National Crisis

The product of extended interdepartmental discussions focusing on the corporate response of The American Lutheran Church to the issues and tensions of the racial and urban crises of 1968, this statement was adopted by the 1968 Convention. Provision was made for a Coordinating Committee on National Crises to implement the objectives and action proposals. This enabling legislation, defining membership and duties, is omitted. Moreover, the 1968 Convention voted "to encourage congregations to establish a Social Concerns Committee."

For Such a Time as This

America is suffering a national crisis. It is a crisis equal to that of 1776, 1861, or 1933. It is a crisis of growing hate, hostility, frustration, and alienation. The crisis grips urban, suburban, and rural America. No race, class, group, institution, section, or segment of America is untouched. So widespread a national crisis calls for clear analysis, resolute choices, and decisive action.

Central in this crisis is a ringing demand for justice and equity in all human relationships. Minorities demand for each person the respect, recognition, freedom, equality, opportunity, and protection due every human being, regardless of his race, religion, national origin, wealth, or any other condition of life. They demand equal justice under law, impartial enforcement of all laws, equality of opportunity, honesty in business dealings, fair prices, just wages, dependable goods and services, and the right to take part in making the decisions that affect them. Lonely voices demand an end to the exploitation, oppression, denial of opportunity, indifference, insensitivity, and the other forms of inhumanity which they see inflicted too often by the strong on the weak. They demand that power be used to effect mercy, equity and opportunity, peace and freedom, righteousness and honor.

A growing recognition of the need for social justice explains efforts to promote better housing and education, sufficient and meaningful jobs, more adequate health and welfare services, and improved relations between the police and citizens. Justice and equity also are at stake in "agricultural parity," "community development," "giving hope to the hopeless," "one man-one vote," "full political participation," the "war on poverty," "tax loopholes and incentives." Justice and equity are involved in "white racism" and "black power," in "selective conscientious objection" and "civil disobedience." Such catchphrases in reality are cries for correction of warped relationships, individual and corporate, which impede the development of justice.

Beneath the surface symptoms of the present crisis lies a deep spiritual disarray. Widespread fear, loneliness, emptiness, and insecurity lead to personally and socially destructive behavior. Self-interest and the desire for power exist within and pose dangers in every group and person. Those who have acquired power or prestige and enjoy its fruits are fearful of the loss of their position. Those on the outside seek access to power and its opportunities, rewards, privileges, and responsibilities. When any group pursues its interests to the hurt or disadvantage of the inherent rights of others, the imbalance causes a crisis of warped relationships. Much "groaning in travail" accompanies the resultant struggle for new relationships

and new structures, the rule of law and justice, and a more equitable
sharing by more groups and persons in the privileges and responsibilities of society.

Today's cries for justice and equity echo Isaiah, Hosea, Amos,
Micah, and the other Old Testament prophets. They call for the
response of discipleship which Jesus described as love, obedience,
and service. They are integral to the witness and work of the
Christian community in its deeds of love active for justice. The
American Lutheran Church takes seriously such Scriptural imperatives as: Do justice . . . abound in love . . . speak truth . . . bear one
another's burdens . . . defend the poor and fatherless . . . relieve the
oppressed . . . show no partiality . . . follow after righteousness
. . . be doers of the word . . . overcome evil with good . . . pray for
one another . . . fear, love, and serve God. Therefore, The American
Lutheran Church must heed and respond to the form and content
which men's cries for recognition and justice take in this time of
national crisis.

Call to Urgent Mission

In this resolute task of heeding and responding to men's cries in
a troubled and suffering world the church must be a decisive partici-
pant. Involvement in concerns for justice inheres in its Christ-given
mission. Human need *is* an arena of Christ's work. Participation in
his work *is* witness. The church's involvement in the struggle for
justice, equity, and mercy portrays parables of God's love in action,
points to signs of the kingdom in our midst, evidences the good
works by which men are drawn to see the Father, and testifies to
its faith by deeds of love active for justice. As the church participates
in the struggle for justice and equity it proclaims with integrity that
God is dynamically renewing and transforming all areas of life. As
it equips its members for their roles in society it extends its influence
into every one of their relationships.

To be true to its trust of preaching the good news of the kingdom
of God and of exemplifying the style of life in the kingdom of God
on earth, The American Lutheran Church must witness to the in-
separability of verbal proclamation from serving deeds of love active
for justice. Its response is one which moves resources into action.
Such a response involves a readiness to experiment and a willingness
to take risks. At its every level of organization the ALC needs to
evidence its genuine interest in and its honest concern for the whole
life of all men, without regard for their wealth, prestige, social

standing, race, political affiliation, or nationality. As the church proclaims the message of redemption and release through the words and deeds of its committed and responsive members it becomes the channel for God's transforming power to change hearts, lives, communities, and the nation.

Identifying Our Objectives

Along with the nation within which it ministers, The American Lutheran Church stands at a time of decision. It must choose resolutely to rededicate itself to its purpose, "the proclamation and propagation of the Christian faith, and the quickening and sanctification of the members of its congregations . . ." (302). It needs renewed emphasis and action on two of the methods to which it is committed: 'Study the problems of contemporary life and society in the light of the word of God, *in order to make its contribution toward solving these problems*" (302.5, emphasis added), and "Develop programs for the promotion of human welfare . . ." (302.6). It claims and proclaims the *whole* gospel for the *whole* man by the *whole* church to the *whole* world.

Toward this end, The American Lutheran Church identifies a number of objectives toward which it must move in responding to the challenge of the national crisis. Through each of these objectives it must seek to influence human lives, to respect the integrity of choices made in the free exercise of human dignity, to manifest the servant role of the church, and to effect needed changes in public opinion and in the structures of secular society. Thus, we identify our mutual need to:

a. Seek understanding, in the light of the Word, of the meaning of crisis events in the nation so that The American Lutheran Church, hearing God's judgments, can respond more effectively to his invitation to commitment, his call to a renewed national life, and the guidance he would give a people in crisis.

b. Increase our sensitivity and response to the human needs and aspirations of minority and economically deprived groups and persons, working with them to secure justice, equity, their share in, and their right to contribute to America's abundance, life, culture, and unity amid diversity.

c. Help build the wholesome attitudes essential to just, equitable, and responsive relationships and structures in society, motivating members of The American Lutheran Church to strive for needed changes in American society, which will bring about a greater measure of justice and equity for all persons.

d. Foster understanding of the potentialition of power to effect change, for good or for evil, and encourage the effective use of power to achieve creative and constructive social purposes.

e. Develop and use with telling moral effect various channels for action through which The American Lutheran Church, as a corporate body at each of its levels of organization and as members active in the structures of society, can participate in constructive movements to cope with the national crisis and its attendant evils.

Channels for Action

Numerous channels are open to The American Lutheran Church for a constructive attack on the crises of urban, suburban, and rural America. As illustrative of the possibilities we propose that The American Lutheran Church should:

a. Intensify efforts to acquaint the unchurched, regardless of their race, nationality, or social standing, with the promises and power of Jesus Christ as Lord and Savior, and to welcome into the participating fellowship of the congregation all who accept his invitation to membership in his church.

b. Increase the level of theological study and understanding, among both pastors and lay persons, of the mission and strategy of the church in an era of rapid and planned social change.

c. Encourage congregations to establish small groups where fellowship and growth in Christian maturity may be nurtured, so as to motivate the members of these congregations for service to their brothers and for service in the structures of society.

d. Undertake an intensive educational effort in The American Lutheran Church to increase understanding of the heritage of minority groups, the dehumanizing nature of racism and poverty, and the relationship of Christian discipleship to justice and equity.

e. Strengthen the supportive services of The American Lutheran Church to its congregations, pastors, agencies, and institutions in the inner city, in dwindling rural communities, and in areas where minority and economically deprived groups and persons are located.

f. Involve minority group persons in the decision-making processes of The American Lutheran Church, and make greater use of minority group persons in the available employment opportunities at each level of The American Lutheran Church as a corporate body.

g. Help formulate and support sound goals of public policy relating to justice and a responsive society, especially focusing critical attention upon legislative, executive, and judicial efforts in the areas of housing, employment, education, welfare, health, and police and law enforcement practices.

h. Use corporate purchasing power to advance racial and social justice by considering the factor of affirmative action for equal employment opportunity as well as quality, cost, and availability of service in contracting for goods, services, and construction.

i. Expand financial and staff support to programs of community action and other cooperative ventures seeking justice and equity, where their aims, objectives, methods, and techniques are deemed by responsible boards, institutions, and units of the church to be compatible with those of The American Lutheran Church.

j. Provide information on effective current programs and projects, and propose specific innovative or experimental programs which can be considered and adopted by groups within The American Lutheran Church, and assist, as resources permit, in the development of such programs and projects.

k. Expand educational opportunities, especially for the recruitment of church workers, through such means as (1) increased scholarships and remedial education programs for minority persons previous to entering and in their studies at the colleges and theological seminaries of The American Lutheran Church and (2) provision for specialized in-service training for those who serve the church in ghettos, poverty areas, and other situations of injustice and inequity.

l. Use investment funds of The American Lutheran Church, its congregations, and institutions, in such enterprises and activities as will benefit minority or economically deprived peoples, to such degree and in such manner as those who bear legal responsibility for these funds may determine.

m. Place priorities on uses of funds which maximize programs and services to people and minimize investment in physical plant and facilities.

n. Cooperate, where possible and in accord with Lutheran theology, with churches and members of all Christian communions in renewal, witness, and service.

Christ for Crises: Hope for All Seasons

In its own decision-making in a time of national crisis The American Lutheran Church has the fortunate opportunity to combine preparations for the celebration of its Tenth Anniversary with a continuation and expansion of Project Summer Hope. The Church Council already has approved a church-wide anniversary theme and emphasis on "Christ for Crises," reaching a crescendo on Pentecost Sunday, 1970, in accord with recommendations of the Commission on Evangelism for that anniversary celebration. This theme and emphasis at the same time can build upon, advance, and expand the dimensions of "Project Summer Hope." This timely project served to deepen and strengthen throughout The American Lutheran Church the foundations of faith, hope, and love, these three with their

obedience, commitment, and readiness to sensitive service. Therefore, we, the delegates to this Fourth General Convention, call for
the combining of preparations for a Tenth Anniversary celebration
and rededication with an enlargement and extension of Project
Summer Hope into a church-wide coordinated focus on "Christ for
Crises: Hope for All Seasons."

We, the delegates to this Fourth General Convention, expect
that the objectives we have identified in paragraph 9 and the channels for action we have proposed in paragraph 10 will be suitably
incorporated into the focus on "Christ for Crises: Hope for All
Seasons." We expect that all units and personnel at the national
offices, and all districts, congregations, institutions, and agencies, will
incorporate into their total work, and witness an appropriate expression of our requested focus on "Christ for Crises: Hope for All
Seasons."

Each district is requested to develop its own focus on "Christ for
Crises: Hope for All Seasons," through which the objectives and
channels for action adopted by this convention can become operative in that district. We look to each district president and executive
committee for leadership in this direction.

Each parish (or neighboring parishes and congregations in joint
action) is requested to take effective steps for implementing in its
own area the objectives and measures of "Christ for Crises: Hope
for All Seasons." Materials and ideas supplied by national district
offices should prove helpful but need not bind or limit local efforts
to fulfill the purposes to which every member congregation of The
American Lutheran Church is bound in mutual commitment.

Openness and Creativity in Response to Crises

In a related action this Convention is called upon to structure and
to delegate authority for crisis action. It is beyond the competence
of this Convention, however, to prescribe the specifics whereby the
several levels and units of The American Lutheran Church can respond to its requested focus on "Christ for Crises: Hope for All
Seasons." It expects each to relate faithfully, openly, and creatively
as its special opportunities and responsibilities permit. Faithful
stewardship of the means of grace, and discipleship in deed and in
truth, permit no retreat from the crises of the world into the
cloisters of ecclesiasticism. A committed people, turned to God
in worship, prayer, and fellowship, must become a responsive
people, their hearts open to the cries of a troubled and suffering

world, their heads and hands working to make love active for justice and equity in all the structures of society.

The current national crisis contains great dangers to, yet also many opportunities for, the future of American society. Discerning choices must be made and wise actions planned in this time of decision. In its own hour of decision, The American Lutheran Church sees the national crisis as infusing its mission with a new dimension of heightened significance. It now commits itself to a renewed dedication and a strengthened obedience, as a servant of Jesus Christ, invoking the Holy Spirit to give it wisdom, power, and perseverance for its task.

Channels for Financial Assistance in Crisis Areas

This statement was adopted by the Joint Council in June 1968 "as a policy statement with respect to financial assistance in programs related to crisis areas."

As members of the congregations become involved in the pursuit of justice for all men, their eagerness to "do something" is understandable. And the fact that "doing something" often involves first the pocketbook is equally understandable.

Eager inquiries have been received from two different sides of the problem. First, from those who are caught up in the midst of tension comes the call "Will the church give us funds to help us meet our metropolitan needs; if not, what can we do about it?" Second, persons and congregations who feel the urgency to assist in this endeavor ask "What are the channels through which we can apply our resources to this need?"

These inquiries suggest the need for a statement of some possible channels through which the church's concern for relieving needs in crisis areas may be expressed, within the polity and framework of its operation.

Preliminarily, we draw attention to several paragraphs of the report of the Board of Trustees to the Joint Council proposing a budget for 1969. An introductory section reads, in part:

Yet the church must remain the church. Though The ALC is circumscribed with historic and traditional geographic, ideological, and theological boundaries, it is at least a part of "the body of Christ." To Christian people, and therefore to the church, has been committed "the word of reconciliation" and "the ministry of reconciliation." It cannot proclaim this word and fulfill this ministry without the tangible demonstration of reconciliation in the relationship of man to man, yet it dare not lose its principal task in its effort to demonstrate the by-product of its principal task.

Other agencies there are, including governments, which must give primary concern for the man-to-man relationship. Christian people are a part of the life stream of those agencies, too, and must direct that they fulfill their responsibilities. The church must support, even inspire, such agencies to fulfill their task aggressively, but the church must not and cannot replace them.

The church has long had a Disaster Relief Fund. Allocations from it have not been recognized as of sufficient size to eliminate a victim's financial burden caused by a natural disaster, such as flood, fire, and earthquake. Rather its purpose has been to show the church's concern for those who are victimized, to fill spirit as much as, usually more than, pocketbook by the tangible demonstration that the church does not "cross by on the other side" and shut its eyes to inordinate need.

It strikes us that the present search for crisis funds is a search for much enlarged Disaster Relief Funds. The crisis is, in a sense, a disaster, brought upon by human elements rather than natural elements. But it, too, is a circumstance which tests the ability of the church to lift spirit, through tangible resources. Perhaps the relativity of the Disaster Fund can be helpful in suggesting the possible channels for the church's expression of concern.

There appear to be three levels of appropriate action:

1. The Local Level

The crisis is, in large part, a "local" matter, even though its multiplicity gives it national proportions. In every community there are specific needs, problems and tensions. A part of the church's concern should be expressed at the local level.

This need not be inconsistent with the ALC polity. It must be carefully recognized that the bylaw prohibitions regarding appeals by boards (1240.1 c), institutions, agencies and "approved Lutheran cooperative agency" (ies) 1240.2 c) and districts (1240.3 c) are all prohibitions against "asking"; they are not to be interpreted as prohibitions upon a congregation or congregations which see a need and desire to relieve it.

Hopefully, congregations particularly in metropolitan areas which cannot be unaware of needs at their doorstep will move to meet those needs by their own voluntary impetus. The ALC Bylaws do not prevent this. But when a few "promoters" attempt to extend such "voluntary" action to all congregations, we have the beginnings

of an "appeal." This is restricted by the ALC Bylaws. In this circumstance, congregations have a right to look to the Board of
Trustees which looks to the appropriate program board, to express
judgment, by its approval or disapproval, upon the appeal, its need,
its urgency, its safeguards.

It is to be expected that in the heat and emotion of personal involvement, individuals or unofficial groups of individuals will bring
strong pressure upon congregations for the use of funds in local
projects. We must maintain a reasonable flexibility in our present
circumstance as to when the communication between congregations
actually becomes an appeal. We can be agreed, we think, that on
the one hand congregations are not restricted in doing that which
they determine to be important in their ministry of reconciliation,
and that on the other hand we have agreed as a group of congregations not to engage in appeals without the approval of the Board
of Trustees, without being forced to the unrewarding and fruitless
exercise of pinpointing the break-over point between them.

Inherent in this distinction is our feeling that the primary reason
for providing for the approval of appeals by the Board of Trustees
is not, as many surmise, the prevention of the erosion of benevolence
funds but rather the right of a congregation to be assured that before it accepts an appeal a responsible group in a "neutral" spot
has evaluated it. This assurance should be preserved. And the
secondary reason of preserving benevolence funds has its merits, too.

Hopefully, too, congregations which respond to local need "voluntarily" will not do so by mere diversion of benevolence funds
from wider to narrower geographic purposes. This only reduces the
ability of the church at other strata to move in the crisis area.
Rather, it is to be hoped that the evidence of the local need will
inspire increased giving.

It might be remembered at this point that when natural disasters
have occurred, the church has not frowned upon the desire of local
congregations and individuals to make direct contributions to the
victims, but recognized such action as a normal reaction of one
who, loved by Christ, loves all for whom Christ died.

2. The District Level

It is not surprising that during the 1968 district conventions several of them took steps to engage in fund-raising activities among
their constituent congregations. The eagerness to "do something"
gets its often least-imaginative, quickest, and cheapest response by

the almost reflex-like action of "voting an appropriation" or "raising a fund." We ought, however, to interpret such action, even if emotion-spawned, as a sincere desire to "do something helpful."

But when such efforts are voted, they seldom appeal only to those who respond with voluntary action but the eagerness of the majority places appeal-type pressure upon the minority. And the pressure becomes stronger if the means adopted is through per capita dues.

It must be recognized that some things can be done more effectively at a level that involves more than a few but less than the national roster of congregations. We see no tendency on the part of the Board of Trustees to overrule a district's desire in this matter if the assurance can be given and substantiated that the desire is more than a spontaneous reaction to emotion, the *modus operandi* is thoughtfully conceived and the result does not linger at the periphery of the problem.

But two cautions ought to be observed by districts. First, such an activity should be recognized as the "appeal" it is, and ought to have the approval of the Board of Trustees and the appropriate program board. The Bylaws provide that this should be "prior approval." It ought to be understood that if the proposal comes to the convention from one of its committees, or if the intention to propose an appeal is known before the convention, the approval should be sought prior to the convention's action. However, recognizing the emotional character of the current circumstance, it is understandable that some such proposals will arise and have arisen spontaneously with no prior planning. The willingness of the Board of Trustees to accept such request after the fact is a part of the flexibility that must mark the day.

True, such a caution can be interpreted at a public gathering as obstructionism, empire-preservation, and decision by those in far away places. But by responsible churchmen, it can also be interpreted as a protective step (since only by the scrutiny of all appeals can the spurious ones be eliminated), as a strengthening step (since concurrence in the effort by those not caught up in the emotion of the decision adds validity to it), and as a coordinating step.

The last thought leads to the second caution. If indeed there is to be financial activity at the local level, the district level, and, as later proposed, the national level, there must be some way of avoiding duplication and multiplicity of effort. A hundred local communities cannot coordinate a district effort; a district can coordinate a hundred local communities. By the same token, 18 districts cannot coordinate a national effort, but a national effort can coordinate 18 district efforts. This is simply to say that districts which engage in such approved programs should be willing to share their efforts and results freely with the national offices, not in the sense of bowing to some higher authority but in eagerness to make the strongest coordinated contribution.

3. The National Level

The American Lutheran Church needs to be involved in demonstrating its concern for the crisis situation. But its concern should not be completely measured by its financial involvement.

The most distinctive contribution the national church can make is in providing ideas and programs. Having on its staff persons who can be presumed to be aware of broad social and economic swings, they can be presumed also to be the earliest alerted and the quickest to react in areas of their competence.

Financially, the ALC will, admittedly, be the slowest of the three levels to react, which ought not be used as criticism but as recognition of fact.

A congregation can move, financially, as quickly as Monday morning after a Saturday decision; such is the nature of its relationship to its members.

A district can move in several weeks after its proposal is approved and the clergy and lay delegates report to their own congregations; such is the nature of its relationship to its congregations.

The ALC has to wait for the next budget year and even then its response is slowed down by having to resort to the less personal channels of communications; such is the nature of its relationship to its congregations.

Yet its financial involvement should not be thought of as inconsequential. Anticipating that a major portion of crisis money will have to come from government, community, and other secular sources, its role can be distinctive in providing seed money in various circumstances. The fact that it is geographically separated from "the local scene" emphasizes an advantage rather than a hindrance, for its decision making can be much freer from the emotional and prejudicial tensions that are present, to a greater or lesser degree, at the other strata.

The question remains whether the ALC can best be involved, financially, with a general crisis fund or with funds allocated to its several departments.

We favor a combination of both, as is proposed by the Board of Trustees for the 1969 budget, recognizing that such a procedure must be recognized as the evident flexibility that marks a crisis circumstance. While the Bylaws appear to assume, though not state, that the church's funds are to be spent under one or another of the boards, there are several reasons why this circumstance can be more effectively met with a common fund:

1. The members of the church apparently want to see and feel that the church is involved. It happens too often that that which is done is hidden from public view when it is all done within a board structure.

2. The nature of the problem is that it overlaps a number of the church's structured boards. A means of providing support without first having to decide "This is American Missions" and "This is Social Service" can speed up the process.

3. Flexibility continues to be a necessary ingredient. It is more easily obtained on an inter-board than an inner-board basis. The board's representatives, nonetheless, who are knowledgeable in these areas ought to maintain the controlling hand to prevent flexibility from becoming chaos.

Some projects, on the other hand, are so evidently within the concerns of one or another of the boards that it would be destructive of efficiency to attempt to forge new channels for their consideration. Hence we do not favor putting all crisis money into an allocatable fund.

4. A Lament for Mr. Smith

We add a fourth level, that of Mr. John Smith, individual churchman. We do so to remind him of his important role in the crisis matter and to remind the church of his frustrating role

Mr. Smith is, at the same time, a member of his congregation, a "member" of his district, and a "member" of the ALC. He may even have a vote in all three strata. In his understandable enthusiasm he may vote crisis programs at all three strata. But Mr. Smith must remember that neither the congregation, the district nor the national church has any money to spend unless he gives it. He must remember that he cannot vote programs he is not willing to support; nor can he vote programs at three levels and then support only two of them. If he tends to impatience with what appears to be insufficient expenditure, he must not be impatient with "them" but with "me" and "us"—the millions of Smiths at his side.

Then the church must remember Mr. Smith's frustrating role—and those in the church who are most eager for statistically impressive activity must remember him. For Mr. Smith is not only a member of a congregation, a district, a church, he is also a resident of a community, a citizen of a state, a contributor to Internal Revenue of the Federal Government. Much of the money he gives, more or less voluntarily, in the latter areas is given for the common good of mankind.

The depression of 1929 changed the role of churches and voluntary agencies. The magnitude of the social task of that day led to the painful and, in some quarters, reluctant conclusion that the church and voluntary agencies were simply not up to the capability of meeting the financial challenges confronting them; only government and public agencies could muster the needed funds quickly enough.

Through the years, the welfare role has been assumed in ever greater proportion by such public enterprises.

Now we face another astronomic financial challenge. That the church should be involved, that its witness should become a public spur, that it takes "seed" to bear "fruit" can hardly be challenged; but that it can suddenly reverse a three-and-a-half decade trend and assume a major role in a crisis similar to one which demonstrated the need of placing the major role in other hands is unlikely.

Let the church be the church. This means it cannot escape involvement in the current crisis. But it also means it cannot be deterred from its commission of proclaiming Christ's word of reconciliation.

Resolution on Current Social Issues

The 1968 Convention acted "To commend the Board of Social Service for the policy it has established to meet current social problems."

In its attempt to participate effectively in meeting current social problems, the board passed a series of resolutions at its meeting of February 1968.

WHEREAS, The Division of Social Service, in keeping with its duties and purposes as expressed in the Constitution of The American Lutheran Church, has always felt a concern about the church meeting the social needs of men in today's society; and

WHEREAS, The Division of Social Service has established a policy whereby innovative services by agencies, congregations, and other segments of the church are to be encouraged within the limitations of budget and staff; and

WHEREAS, The Social Service agencies of the church often have on their staffs persons with the necessary competence to help congregations in meeting the social needs of men, sometimes also having limited resources to devote to such work; and

WHEREAS, The Division of Social Service believes that the church must become more involved in and concerned about the present social situation; and

WHEREAS, Numerous communications have come to the Division of Social Service from congregations, districts, groups of pastors, individuals, and from The American Lutheran Church itself for help from the Division of Social Service in meeting the problems of our times; now therefore be it

Resolved, That the Board of Social Service declare again that it stands ready to be of service to the church in meeting current social crises within the limitations of its staff and budget, and be it further

Resolved, That the Division of Social Service encourage its agencies to be alert to total social needs in their respective communities and strive to do what they can to meet crisis situations; and be it further

Resolved, That the Division of Social Service pledge its full cooperation to other divisions of the church in this effort; and be it further

Resolved, That the Division of Social Service ask for consideration by The American Lutheran Church of a request for special additional funds to be made available to the Division of Social Service, the Division of American Missions, the Commission on Research and Social Action, and any other division of the church which may have on its staff competent personnel for giving leadership in meeting social crises, in order that The American Lutheran Church can assist congregations and agencies of the church in the area of social concerns.

Combatting Communism

"Approved as a policy statement by the Church Council, The American Lutheran Church, October 1961 on recommendation of the Commission on Research and Social Action."

The steadily growing menace of international communism and the dangers this causes for national security have placed congregations and members in many portions of our church under strong pressure to join crusades or organizations to combat communism or to lend their facilities to combat communism.

This pressure calls for clear thinking as to the purpose of the church. The "United Testimony on Faith and Life," adopted by our uniting churches in 1952, has two paragraphs which speak to the kind of situation facing us. (*Handbook of the ALC*, page 178):

> We believe that in this world of sin and strife where the forces of evil are threatening to destroy both the church and society, the Lord of the church is summoning his people to dedicate themselves, their possessions, and all their powers anew to the accomplishment of his saving purposes for mankind. Following the example of our Lord Jesus Christ, the church seeks and works for the complete well-being of all men.
>
> All men must be made to recognize the authority of God's law to which they are responsible and by which they are judged. Those in authority in all areas of life must govern according to God's law which is ordained for the ordering of human society and the welfare of all. So governing, they are instruments of God and servants of the common good. Failing to do so they bring God's judgment upon themselves and destruction and disaster to the society which they govern.

Thus judged, Marxist-Leninist communism, whether in Russia, its satellites, or China, must be condemned. It denies the triune God, and divorces man from divinely intended fellowship with his creator. It breeds not love but hate. It sees man not as a person but as a thing, expecting him to serve the state rather than the state to serve him. Truth is a concept it neither knows nor practices. It employs any means, however ruthless, cynical, or deceitful, to gain its ends. Its end is the total allegiance—heart, mind, soul, and body—of all who come under its power.

Every American Christian, living in a land of religious freedom, of respect for the person, and of other civil liberties guaranteed him, stands opposed to the conspiracy of international communism which would bring the whole world under the rule of Marxist-Leninist doctrines. We believe that this would "bring God's judgment upon themselves and destruction and disaster to the society which they governed." Yet, totally rejecting the system, we still share in God's love for people living under it.

At issue, then, is not the position we take, but the methods we use. FBI Director J. Edgar Hoover, in *Masters of Deceit* (Cardinal Giant edition, p. 290) points out one method to avoid:

> Smears, character assassination, and the scattering of irresponsible charges have no place in this nation. They create division, suspicion, and

distrust among loyal Americans—just what the communists want—and hinder rather than aid the fight against communism.

Congregations and church members could well endorse and participate in methods such as these:

Study—of communist ideology and methods and of our own Christian and democratic heritage, using the established organizations within the congregation and making sure to maintain balance, objectivity, and sound scriptural perspective in such study;

Developing bonds of companionship and understanding—especially with youth, members of the armed forces, members of minority or disadvantaged groups, and newcomers and foreigners in our communities;

Responsible action—including avoiding being duped into communist or "front" organizations, resisting possible efforts to "take over" legitimate causes, reporting to the FBI what appear to be attempts at espionage, sabotage, or other subversive activities, and remedying conditions of discrimination or injustice which may make persons susceptible to the lures of communism;

Clarifying and emphasizing positive goals—to which persons readily can give their devotion and energies, genuinely serving "the complete well-being of all men" in our nation and in the emerging nations, and avoiding negative emphases on mere self-preservation, maintenance of the status quo, or narrow nationalism.

Consistently in their study, work, and witness on the communism issue pastors, congregations, and members should make two points crystal clear:

1) whatever noble goals or attractive social ideals communism may profess actually are already inherent in the underlying principles of democracy and have their roots in Christianity;

2) as in all other areas of social living, the church best serves the nation and creates the proper attitude toward fellow men and toward government when it unfailingly proclaims the whole Word of God and practices conscientious pastoral care of souls.

As a church we are dedicated to the accomplishment of God's "saving purpose for mankind." In deciding whether to join local organizations or causes combatting communism, church councils and members of our congregations are urged to evaluate not merely the declared objectives but particularly the methods used. Congregations would be wise to refrain from formal participation or official encouragement unless it is inescapably plain that this will be a means for furthering God's "saving purposes for mankind."

B. CHRISTIANS IN POLITICAL LIFE

Christians in Politics

1966 Convention action: "Resolved, That The American Lutheran Church adopt the following statement on 'Christians in Politics' as an encouragement to its members to engage wholeheartedly as Christians in the processes of politics by which their communities, states, and nation are governed."

Christians inescapably are citizens of a temporal realm. "Subject to the governing authorities," Christians see government as God's agent to accomplish his purposes of justice, equity, righteousness, protection of the disadvantaged, curbing of evil, and the other beneficial qualities of civic life. (See Ps. 82; Prov. 8:15, 16; Rom. 13:1-7; 1 Pet. 2:13-14.)

Christians living in a democracy just as inescapably are involved in politics. In their offices as citizens Christian people share responsibility for governmental decisions and public policies. Even when they remain silent or do nothing Christians act as citizens. They act to delegate their citizenship responsibilities to persons who do speak up and who do act through the processes of politics to shape the laws and structures of society.

Too many Christians regard politics as dirty or divorced from their faith. The church needs to correct this false idea. Politics is the way in which power is organized, conflict is controlled, public policy is developed. Politics is simply the process of community decision-making. Politics is a necessary and wholesome part of man's civic life, under God's sustaining hand.

To the Christian service in the public sphere is a channel through which to express a part of his call from God. Politics can be the arena in which he becomes God's light, Christ's salt, and the Spirit's leaven for a better community, closer to the kind of society the Creator designed.

Since politics is an activity exercised largely through political parties or nonpartisan civic action groups, Christians need to become active workers in political parties and civic action committees. Thereby they can help to influence the selection of candidates, support candidates and office holders, define issues, propose goals for public policy, develop programs of governmental action, and foster informed voting. This basic work of politics begins with dedicated activity at the precinct level.

The goal of the Christian in politics is to exercise an enlightened

Christian citizenship that strives for the well-being of the total community. He remains alert not to use his political power and influence to advance the corporate concerns of his own church or to make its dogma binding upon others. He respects the fact that differences in political persuasion do and should exist within a church, in whose fellowship and pastoral relationship all should feel themselves one in Christ.

Compromise is an inevitable part of the give and take of politics. Compromise involves the process of achieving a meeting of the minds, an acceptable consensus, a workable reconciliation of conflict—or of diverse views. Such compromise moves toward wholesome, mutually desired goals. It accepts the possible as a step toward the desirable. Seen in this light compromise can be an expression of Christian respect for persons and community. It may require one to yield some of his own advantage for the sake of others and the good of the community.

The Christian will find that citizenship action requires sacrifice. He will experience criticism, abuse, misinterpretation of his words and actions, and financial burdens. He may find it necessary to run for office or espouse causes even when he is sure to lose. Yet, offsetting the sacrifices, he can find genuine satisfactions in a calling conscientiously performed to the glory of God and the good of neighbor and community.

Outwardly the political involvement of the Christian differs little from that of his non-Christian neighbor. Indeed, the two can and must work closely together. The practice of politics has no uniquely Christian properties. The Christian in politics does differ, however, in the spiritual resources available to him, his motivations to service, his attitudes toward other people, his reasons for the goals to which he commits himself, his understanding of human failure, and his experience of the reality of grace and forgiveness.

A Christian involved in bureaucratic decision-making processes, wherein a few persons make decisions vital to millions, often feels frustrations of helplessness. For his part he may have prepared information, analyses, or recommendations pertinent to the issue, but which were not accepted. He realizes that choices had to be made between conflicting value systems and opposing viewpoints. Unless he feels keenly that urgent moral or other overriding considerations were violated he accepts the decision and lives within the bureaucratic controls. Should he feel the issue keenly enough, however, he must use the built-in processes for appeal and review of the decision. Or, he must resign his office to disassociate himself from concurrence in the decision.

The corporate church expresses its support for political processes and governmental servants through intercessory prayers, teaching, counsel, study and discussion groups, and constructive suggestions for the shaping of public policy. Its schools and colleges encourage and prepare persons for informed service in politics. Whether specific issues and candidates should be supported or opposed is a matter best left to specific decision in light of immediate political realities and current social situations.

The corporate church needs to correct false distinctions often made between sacred and secular, spiritual and earthly. The church and its members inescapably are involved in politics. Politics is the process by which men exercise God's grant of his authority to foster whatever is good and to curb whatever is evil in society. The influence of the church and its members needs always to be an enlightening and leavening witness for honesty, integrity, justice, truth, wholeness in the community, and the other ingredients basic to a sound society.

Ministry of the Laity

The following resolution, submitted by the General Convention Committee, was adopted by the 1970 convention.

Whereas, The witness and ministry of the Christian layman in his daily life and work is a vital and significant part of the work of the church in the world; and

Whereas, The witness and ministry of the layman should be affirmed and strengthened by the church; therefore be it

Resolved, That every effort should be made to help the Christian layman to recognize and better understand that he can serve and is serving his church as a servant of God through his witness and ministry to others in his daily work; and be it further

Resolved, That the church not only recognize and affirm such ministry of the layman, but that it also provide opportunities and strong encouragement for continuing education and training to equip him for such ministry.

The Peace Corps

1962 Convention action adopted the following resolution, referred to the General Convention for consideration after having been adopted at the 1962 annual meeting of the National Lutheran Council.

WHEREAS, The Peace Corps has been established by the United States government "to help the people of interested countries and areas in meeting their needs for skilled manpower" as well as "to promote a better understanding of the American people on the part of the peoples served and a better understanding of other peoples on the part of the American people"; and

WHEREAS, The Peace Corps provides a creative opportunity for citizens of good will and competence to serve human need, and to demonstrate the power of disciplined service given without prospect of pecuniary advantage; and

WHEREAS, The Christian's call into the fellowship of the church is at the same time a call to active participation, under the sign of the cross, in the world recognized as a realm in which God is active in creation, judgment, and redemption; now therefore be it

Resolved, That The American Lutheran Church:

1. Register its general endorsement of the objectives of the Peace Corps.

2. Commend the president and the Congress for the inauguration of a Peace Corps program which has already given evidence of high standards of performance.

3. Commend the administration of the Peace Corps for its announced policy of not approving churches and religious agencies as sponsors of Peace Corps projects and express hope that this policy will be maintained.

4. Encourage qualified Lutherans to participate in the Peace Corps program as a significant opportunity for service.

1968 Convention action adopted the following resolution submitted by an individual delegate:

Resolved, That we recognize the work of the lay apostolate of God's people from The American Lutheran Church, young and old, in the Peace Corps of the U.S.A., that we accept the witness of their work and involvement in the world of nations as churchmanship and mission even though their proclamation is not in the word of the gospel but in its works, and that we point to this opportunity for selfless devotion as Christlike commitment of the strong to the plight of the weak.

C. THE PASTOR'S ROLE

The Role of the Pastor in the Community

A statement on this question was submitted to the 1968 Convention by the Commission on Research and Social Action. It drew such fire from two sides—that it went too far and that it did not go far enough—that the Convention returned the statement to the Commission for further study. The revised draft, taking account of re-

sponses received from the field, was endorsed by the Church Council and adopted by the 1970 Convention as "a policy statement of The American Lutheran Church, normative for governing the corporate decisions and actions of all units of The American Lutheran Church."

The Lutheran heritage allows each generation to decide, on prudential consideration within the Christian fellowship, in what particular manner pastors should relate their ecclesiastical and their civic activities. It does not prescribe any specific forms for the life of the pastor-citizen. It affirms the rule of God over all of life. It distinguishes God's work through the means of grace from his activity through civic institutions. It also identifies specific functional responsibilities central to the office of pastor.

The office of pastor is only *functionally* different from the responsibility of any other Christian; it exists for the sake of good order in the household of faith. The pastor's special responsibility is for encouraging, training, and equipping the laity for *their* ministry in the community. While the congregation as the people of God is called to be servant, priest, and prophet in the community, the pastor has a special leadership role in these expressions of mission. The pastor's ecclesiastical functions vary according to time and place, but traditionally his central functions have been preaching, administration of the sacraments, teaching, and counseling (cf. Augsburg Confession XXVIII). Most other activities are by the personal choice of the pastor and are not peculiar to this office.

The pastor should be as free to participate in community activities as any lay Christian or any other citizen. As such, he is entitled to the same rights and is responsible for the same duties as any other citizen (cf. "Christians in Politics," *Reports and Actions,* 1966, pp. 487-489). State laws, nevertheless, usually exempt him from jury duty and may respect privileged communications due to the nature of his profession. Many persons, however, find it difficult to distinguish the pastor's civic activities from his ecclesiastical responsibilities. The confusion is most evident when pastors become involved in specifically political affairs, including stands on public issues, partisan political participation, endorsement of candidates, and seeking or holding public office. Therefore, in any civic action the pastor should take into account his many relationships and responsibilities. As any other citizen he should evaluate how positive effects in certain areas might outweigh negative effects elsewhere as a result of his activities.

It is nevertheless proper and desirable for the pastor to take an informed and active part in civic affairs. The American Lutheran Church encourages its pastors to participate in civic activities. Such activity can include the full range of endeavors, including participation in civic organizations, political activity, community organization, and even movements to change the course of public policy. Civic participation allows the pastor to assume the responsibilities and to exercise the rights of active citizenship. It can help him better to understand life as his people experience it, thus improving his pastoral effectiveness. It becomes a public expression of his and the congregation's concern for the well-being of the whole community.

Indeed there may be times and circumstances when the pastor must act as the public representation of Christian conscience. When others through their lack of concern permit the perpetuation of injustice, it may be necessary for the pastor, in his sensitivity to Christ's mission, to show his congregation and the community through his deeds the meaning of God's word for men's lives. In his commitment to and struggle for social justice the pastor remains aware of how congregation and community interpenetrate and influence one another.

In his private activities as a citizen, the pastor should make plain the personal character of his views and actions. He should be open and candid with his congregation as to the reasons underlying his actions. He should seek to avoid alienating his congregation or jeopardizing his pastoral relations with members by excessive partisanship on economic, political, or social issues. He should not use the pulpit for strictly partisan causes. He should enlist the knowledge, wisdom, and counsel of others before embarking on a course of action which threatens to impair the effectiveness of his ministry. He should be particularly careful not to use the weight of his office to reinforce his own personal views.

The pastor should not expect any special privileges from the community because of his status as a pastor. Such privileges may demean the office and person of the pastor as well as the integrity of the church's mission. The pastor must remember that the office of pastor bestows no special competence on public issues or matters of public policy; he participates in civic life on the same basis as any other citizen. In order to emphasize this he may find it wise to forego wearing clergy apparel on certain occasions. At the same time he is as much obligated as is any other public figure to be informed on an issue before he speaks or acts in public on that issue.

These considerations are in no wise meant to deter the pastor from speaking or acting in the community. On the contrary, The American Lutheran Church, as noted earlier, encourages civic participation both as a dimension of citizenship and as an avenue of Christian life. This statement suggests some of the considerations which should guide pastors in determining their particular courses of action and forms of involvement in the community. At the same time, this statement suggests considerations which should guide congregations in honoring the activities in which their pastors engage as responsible members of the community.

A pastor currently may be uninvolved, underinvolved, or overinvolved in civic activities. Periodically the church council should consult with the pastor in evaluating his role and effectiveness in the community. The example and influence of the pastor who participates with knowledge and conviction in the work of the community is a powerful testimony to the relevance of the gospel. To be sure, both pastor and congregation need to exercise discretion. Wise counsel for difficult decisions in community life is expressed in 1 Peter 2:10: "Maintain good conduct among the Gentiles, so that in case they speak against you as wrongdoers, they may see your good deeds and glorify God on the day of visitation."

Public Endorsement of Political Candidates

The Church Council in 1968 "adopted the following statement in response to questions regarding clergy endorsement of political candidates."

The Church Council calls attention to the statement already adopted by the Third General Convention of The American Lutheran Church (1966) entitled *Christians in Politics,* as an encouragement to its members to engage wholeheartedly as Christians in the process of politics by which their communities, states, and nation are governed.

The Church Council recommends that teachers, pastors, or staff members in the service of The American Lutheran Church refrain from attaching to their own names the name of the congregation or institution they serve when, or if, they publish statements in support of political candidates. They should rather be identified only by their own name and home address.

D. GUIDELINES FOR PROGRAM PLANNING

The 1968 Convention, acting on a report from the Long Range Study Committee, adopted the following, "Resolved, That The American Lutheran Church adopt the following Broad Guidelines for Program Planning and establish these broad guidelines as normative for determining the actions of congregations, districts, conferences, institutions and agencies, and councils, boards, commissions, and committees of The American Lutheran Church."

Declare and evidence its commitment to total Lutheran unity, moving as rapidly as possible in inter-Lutheran cooperation and fellowship. Participate in interchurch and ecumenical projects and Christian witness as circumstances warrant.

Foster congregational cooperation and concern for sister congregations, including organization of federated parishes, development of joint programs, the sharing of specialized personnel, greater use of the mass media, and a more comprehensive ministry to the total community in which the congregations are serving.

Encourage common staff, wherever possible, for district or metropolitan areas jointly with LCA or LC-MS, recognizing that the necessity of ministering amid common community circumstances may unite the area congregations in close ties of fellowship and service.

Encourage soundly conceived and carefully observed experimental ministries and innovative techniques which promise to advance the purposes to which the ALC is committed.

Identify and foster the specialized role and functions of the pastor both as a person of theological competence and as the possessor of insights and skills unique in the community for equipping the saints.

Identify and make more effective use of the specialized knowledge and skills of the laity in the mission and ministry of the church, including its internal organization, administration, program development, witness and service in the community.

Develop lay training programs for vocational groups, both men and women, to equip them the better for their ministry in society, including their opportunities as members of the body of Christ to serve the non-Christians with whom they come in contact at home and abroad.

Place increased reliance upon the strengths and commitment of small core groups within the congregations, their members dedicated to the purpose and mission of the church and giving of themselves in love and service far beyond that expected of the bulk of the membership.

Provide for conference, district, and national office flexibility and openness to respond to emerging opportunities, placing responsibility and authority for decision making, consistent with corporate policies.

Clarify administrative lines and consolidate ALC structures and operations in accord with sound organizational principles, identifying responsibility, accountability, and authority at each functional level. Protect the healthy tension of an effective system of checks and balances. Recognize the tension between the shepherding or pastoral and the legislative or administrative functions.

Make enlarged and telling use of the multiple channels of communication within the interacting networks of the ALC, building basically upon primary, person-to-person confrontation rather than upon secondary, impersonal contacts.

Establish structures and procedures by which the ALC systematically can evaluate its performance and effect needed coordination and comprehensive long-range plans, including the termination of programs and units which have outlived their usefulness.

III

Church-State Relations

A. A BASIC STANCE

The following statement was adopted by two general conventions. 1964 Convention action: "Resolved, That The American Lutheran Church commend the following statement on 'Church-State Relations in the U.S.A.' to the members of the church in order to stimulate their thinking and to promote their discussion of the issues." Two years later, 1966 Convention action adopted the following:

WHEREAS, The statement on "Church-State Relations in the U.S.A.," commended by the General Convention of 1964 has been widely circulated and favorably received; therefore be it

Resolved, That the 1966 General Convention accept this statement as an expression of the policy and conviction of The American Lutheran Church on the issues treated therein.

Introduction

Numerous issues affecting church-state relations, the place of religion in public life, and the recognition of deity by government, have entered the arena of public debate. The issues have arisen in large part because of the increased heterogeneity of the American population, the acceptance of religious pluralism, the extension of governmental influence into nearly every phase of life, the need for additional tax revenues, and the difficulties for the churches in meeting the growing demands and complexities of their programs of health, education, and welfare.

47

We recognize that Scripture gives only guidelines, not blue-prints for determining church-state relations. The charge given the church to make disciples of all men (Matt. 28:16-20), the power given government to support good and to curb evil (Rom. 13:1-7), the separation between that which is owed to God and to government (Matt. 22:15-22), and the direction of the Christian's influence in society (Mark 12:28-34) remain basic for all generations. The specific ways of fostering and protecting these essentials, however, may and do differ from age to age and from nation to nation.

Speaking as American Christians to the members of The American Lutheran Church who live in the United States, we express the following views in order to stimulate their thinking, and to promote their discussion of the issues.

In referring to the *church* we include those legal corporate entities which seek to accomplish the specific religious purposes to which they are committed. By the *state* we mean all units of government which exercise political authority, whether at the local, state, or national levels.

A Heritage of Religious Pluralism

Included in the American heritage is a recognition that man and the nation live under God. As a nation our highest appeal traditionally, as in the Declaration of Independence, is to "the Laws of Nature and of Nature's God." The phrase "this nation, under God," spoken by President Lincoln at Gettysburg in 1863, expresses the loyalty of millions of his countrymen, both those who preceded and those who followed him. The phrase "In God We Trust" on our coins, and the presidential proclamation of a day of Thanksgiving, we believe fall within this heritage of voluntary religious expression.

While we confess our loyalty to the triune God, made known to us through Jesus Christ, we acknowledge that a practical level of civic righteousness may be achieved by rational men without conscious reference to deity. We hold, however, that man's way of life and man's highest good are best protected when seen in the perspective of eternally true moral values or divine purposes, as when the people of a nation affirm "that all men are created equal, that they are endowed by their Creator with certain unalienable rights, that among these are life, liberty, and the pursuit of happiness."

Religious pluralism has developed under and is protected in the American heritage. The Constitution denies to government the right to interfere with the person's exercise of his religion, provided that he does not offend public decency or tread upon the rights of others. The Constitution prohibits making any religion an established religion. It forbids setting up a religious test as a qualification for public office. The Constitution favors no one religion over another.

It follows, therefore, that government must steer a difficult course of benevolent neutrality. It should not, in its policies, discriminate against the institutions of religion, nor should it impose obstacles and burdens which hinder persons in the responsible exercise of their religion. It must protect the freedoms alike of the religious citizens and those who practice no religion. Government has an obligation to foster a climate conducive to the free exercise of religion, to give equal protection to all religious views, and to express its neutrality in terms of actions the probable consequences of which it has carefully weighed.

The Separation of Church and State

Both church and state, each in its own way and using methods appropriate to its own function, are to be instruments for accomplishing God's purposes. Our concern is that the church be free to be the church, the state to be the state, each true to its own God-ordained functions. The state, in the performance of its God-given mandate, may not recognize its authority as coming from God but Christians in any event will so see the authority of government.

Essentially the church is God's avenue for reconciling man to himself and for bearing living witness to his divine truth for man's life in community. The state is his instrument for maintaining peace, order, and justice in the community, for protecting the individual's rights, for enhancing his possibilities for personal development, and thus for promoting the general welfare.

The church makes its presence effective through changes wrought in persons by the Holy Spirit, working through the Word and the sacraments, to effect the dynamics of spiritual growth. The state makes its presence effective through its authority, under law, to pre-empt property and goods, labor, even life, into its service and through the response of identification and loyalty of its citizens.

The church looks to the state to maintain the kind of civil order that assures peace, justice, and responsible freedom. As a corporate body the church operates under the laws of the state. Nevertheless, the church retains the right and the duty to proclaim the prophetic

Word of God even in opposition to policies of government which are in conflict with the Word. The church counsels its members under every circumstance to obey the laws enacted by the governing authorities except in the rare event that the demands of men's laws conflict with the Christian's higher loyalty to God.

Interrelation of Church and State

Both church and state, under God, serve genuine needs of human beings. In so doing, they mutually affect one another. Neither should surrender its independence to the other, nor perform functions exclusively appropriate to the other. Church and state complement one another as they devote themselves to the best interests and well-being of persons.

Toward this end churches motivate interest in and respect for laws basic to civic righteousness and beneficial to the wholeness of the community. Christian churches derive the authority for and the principles of their witness on proposed legislation from God's Word with its teachings, for example, on sin, justice, love, and truth and its counsel to rulers. In any testimony they give to the governing authorities churches ought not leave the impression that they seek to exercise legislative powers over the community or that they possess particular political wisdom. Rather, they ought to stress in their public witness the effects of proposed courses of action both upon persons and upon such values of a free society as

—impartial justice and equity,

—honesty and integrity,

—respect for person, property, and authority,

—the exercise of responsible freedom,

—a balancing of the needs of the person with the claims of the community, and

—a recognition that government exercises a positive role in human affairs.

In its practical operation the American heritage generally has embodied a flexible pattern of cooperation between church and state in providing for persons such services as are deemed to be in the public interest and for the good of the community. Neither indifference, nor hostility, nor a wall of separation but a flexible friendly cooperation to achieve what is agreed as being for the common good has marked church-state relationships in America. This has been especially true in the areas of education, welfare services, and ministries to persons in institutions and the armed forces.

Danger exists for both church and state in too-close an identification with the programs of each. Governmental grants, loans, and other forms of assistance to religious institutions indeed may enable the churches the more effectively to serve the needs of an expanding society. Such governmental assistance may also, on the other side, compromise the religious character of the institution and jeopardize its essential integrity. What may be good for government may be harmful to the church, or vice versa. One or a few religious groups may be strengthened to the disadvantage of others. Governmental policies may be determined by one or another strong religious group to its own temporal advantage.

The state should not by its actions or inaction show preference for any religious viewpoint. Otherwise, community divisiveness may be intensified, religious animosities may be created, and antireligious attitudes may be fostered. On the other hand, the state, while not directly supporting or compelling religious teachings or practices, should be free to condition the exercise of its coercive powers and be ready to adjust its programs in deference to the religious freedom and the religious expression of the people.

Neutrality and Equal Protection

It is unwise to establish blanket endorsements or blanket repudiations of particular forms of cooperative endeavors between church and state. Each must be evaluated in terms of its own merits and demerits, the precedents it sets, the probable consequences which will follow either acceptance or refusal of cooperative endeavor, and whether the action jeopardizes the freedom of either church or state to fulfill its God-given functions.

It may be questioned whether in a country as large and as diverse culturally as is the United States it is wise to attempt to impose by judicial decision uniform rules and tests applicable to every governmental unit at all levels, respecting all practices that may be seen to involve some aspect of church-state relations. It should be a matter of central concern that basic constitutional freedoms of race, religion, and conscience are protected, but short of this the solution to the many specific problems involving church-state relations is better left to the states and localities. Many such practical problems can be resolved locally by discussion and compromise by the various interested groups without resort to the courts and the processes of litigation.

We respect, nevertheless, the conscientious convictions of those who believe it necessary to appeal to the courts to protect their basic rights, and we affirm the duty of the courts to decide such issues in protection of fundamental human liberties.

Applications to Some Specifics

For government to give place and support to the chaplaincy ministry in the armed forces, in correctional institutions, and in governmental hospitals for the long-term care and treatment of patients is both a valid exercise of governmental interest in the whole person and an example of the religious neutrality of the state. Government for its purposes has removed these persons from the normal freedoms of community life and from the normal congregational ministry of the church. It witnesses to its concern for religious liberty and the free exercise of religion when it provides opportunity for a spiritual ministry to persons totally in its care. The state properly should exercise reasonable administrative controls over those who provide this spiritual ministry, while protecting their right to minister according to the dogma and practices of their ecclesiastical tradition.

Benefits to which the person is entitled through statute by reason of citizenship, residence, need, special service, or unusual ability should not be denied or limited because he chooses to use the services of agencies and institutions of the church rather than those of government. Old age assistance grants, medical payments, hot lunches, grants for dependent children, higher educational benefits, and health and safety education are examples of such benefits to persons.

Any form of direct public support for educational institutions under religious auspices jeopardizes the religious freedom of persons who are not members of that religious body. It compels them to support the indoctrination of religious views which they do not share. We believe that to provide bus transportation or school textbooks at public expense for children enrolled in parochial schools is fraught with such divisive consequences that it is contrary to good public policy. We urge, however, that debate on the effects of public policy in these sensitive areas upon the respective interests of religious bodies should not cause Christian people to neglect their proper concern for the well-being of children, regardless of their religious affiliation.

Policies Respecting Taxation

Tax policies should encourage personal contributions to voluntary, not-for-profit, organizations of a charitable, health, educational, or religious character. The community needs strong organizations of this type, alike for their positive values, to avoid total reliance upon governmental agencies, and for the mutually healthy and corrective influence between governmental and voluntary agencies. The freedom of the individual citizen to exercise his personal philanthropy and generously to support constructive voluntary enterprises of his own choice ought to be protected in the public interest.

Tax exemption of church buildings owned and used directly and solely for worship, educational, and eleemosynary purposes is a sound exercise of public policy. It recognizes the contributions the church and its institutions make to community life. To levy upon churches nondiscriminatory charges for municipal services such as water, sewage, police, and fire protection we believe is an action consistent with sound public policy. We believe that the churches should be willing to accept equitable taxation of parsonages and other dwellings owned by churches, associations of churches, or religious orders in which their staff members reside.

Churches owning properties and conducting business not exclusively and solely essential to their religious, charitable, or educational ministry ought to be subject to tax laws and policies equally applicable to those governing profit-seeking individuals, partnerships, and corporations.

Religion in the Schools

Reading of Scripture and addressing deity in prayer are forms of religious expression which devout persons cherish. To compel these religious exercises as essential parts of the public school program, however, is to infringe on the distinctive beliefs of religious persons as well as on the rights of the irreligious. We believe that freedom of religion is best preserved when Scripture reading and prayer are centered in home and church, their effects in the changed lives of devout persons radiating into the schools and into every area of community life. It is as wrong for the public schools to become agents of atheism, godless secularism, scoffing irreligion, or a vague "religion in general" as it is for them to make religious rites and ceremonies an integral part of their programs.

It is a distortion of the constitutional principle of neutrality of the state toward religion to insist that public schools ignore the influence of religion upon culture and persons. A rounded education ought to include knowledge of major religious groups and their emphases, the influence of religion upon the lives of people, and the contributions of religion to society, taught in history, literature, social science, and other courses at levels consistent with the maturity and comprehension of the pupils. The objective for the public schools in this direction is understanding rather than commitment, a teaching *about* religion rather than a teaching *of* religion. Churches ought to offer their assistance to the public schools in preparing for and in supporting the teaching of such courses.

Whether and how disinctive religious holidays should be recognized in the public schools, and whether public property may be used for religious displays and ceremonies, we believe are matters best decided by the responsible authorities in each community in light of (a) the interests and desires of the people of that community, (b) government's obligation to benevolent neutrality in religious matters, (c) the protections and opportunities for redress guaranteed any minorities, and (d) the possibility that the religious significance of the holiday will be lost as it becomes simply a seasonal rite or ceremony.

Released time, dismissed time, and shared time are means deserving of greater exploration so that the churches can give religious education, competently and in accord with their distinctive doctrinal emphases, to pupils enrolled in the public schools. Such programs would require rejection of the dogmatic and inflexible approach fostered by the slogan "separation of church and state." Such study might result in encouraging genuinely benevolent neutrality on the part of government and a fresh approach to the free exercise of religion in education not otherwise attainable.

Further Lutheran Action

Lutheran congregations should guide and support their members in their participation as citizens in shaping governmental decisions. They should encourage, help, and strengthen their members to exert an effective influence as Christians in the political life of the nation. All of life lived under God possesses for the Christian a unity, spirituality, and sacredness. It is this conviction which Lutheran congregations and their members need to re-emphasize in discussion of the proper relations between church and state.

While we dare not surrender our prophetic office, as a Lutheran church we normally do not seek to tell governing authorities how they should govern, or to prescribe the specific details of the laws they should pass. This task we leave to the enlightened, sensitive consciences of citizens and public officials, many of them our brethren in the faith. Our task as a church is to speak the whole counsel of God to our members, helping them thereby, with the power of the Holy Spirit, to be better informed, sensitively Christian citizens actively working for a better community, nation, and world. Respect for law and authority . . . the reign of impartial justice and equity . . . acceptance of the blessings and obligations of citizenship . . . vigilance to preserve for all men their inalienable human freedoms and liberties . . . opportunities for the free exercise of religion . . . recognition of man's responsibilities both to himself and to his neighbors . . . these are among the elements essential to this better community, nation, and world.

A particularly valuable, carefully prepared, currently relevant booklet meriting widespread study is *Church and State: A Lutheran Perspective*, issued in 1963 by the Board of Social Ministry of the Lutheran Church in America, reporting the conclusions of a special Commission on Church and State Relations in a Pluralistic Society, which included in its membership two members of The American Lutheran Church.

B. FUNDS FOR CHURCH INSTITUTIONS

The Church Council in 1961 elected a special committee "to study the use of federal funds for institutions" of social service and higher education, and charged the committee "to submit a policy statement for the consideration of the General Convention." This committee submitted the following report on "Principles Guiding Acceptance of Federal Aid to Church Institutions," which was adopted by the 1962 Convention.

General Foreword

The Constitution of The American Lutheran Church, in Article III, Section 2, states that: "The specific purpose of The American Lutheran Church is the proclamation and propagation of the Christian faith, and the quickening and sanctification of the members of its congregations through the use of the means of grace."

The same section then proceeds to enumerate nine areas in which the church accepts responsibility for the accomplishment of its purpose. Among these, Numbers 3, 4, 5, and 6 have relevance for the purposes of this document. They are:

3. Assist the congregations in the nurture of the children, youth, and adults in the covenant of their Baptism that they may grow in Christian faith and life.

4. Establish, develop, maintain, and operate theological seminaries, colleges, and other educational institutions.

5. Study the problems of contemporary life and society in the light of the word of God, in order to make its contribution toward solving these problems.

6. Develop programs for the promotion of human welfare, and establish, maintain, support, or operate health and welfare institutions and agencies.

By its commitment to faith in Jesus Christ, and by adopting the Constitution with this statement of purpose, The American Lutheran Church has committed itself and its members to these responsibilities. These responsibilities bring the church into spheres of activity in which secular society also is operating, and provoke, at these points, a potential conflict with the principle of the separation of church and state, as enunciated in the Constitution of the United States.

At these points of potential conflict the church must remember that it has assumed these responsibilities, whether or not it receives cooperation or support from the government. And, the church, as the body of Christ, must always remember that its commitment to the command of its Lord as expressed in its purpose requires sacrifice. The church must never consent to cheapen its awareness of the cost of its own redemption by expecting an unredeemed society to carry the burden which rightfully belongs to the church alone. The claim of Christ upon his church in this respect is clearly stated in his own words: "If any man would be my disciple, let him deny himself and take up his cross and follow me" (Mark 8:34).

Foreword to this Document

In relation to the question of federal aid to church institutions, therefore, the church must be aware constantly that it stands in danger of being limited or restricted in some way, or at some time, in its freedom to fulfill some part of its purpose as it interprets the Lord's command. This hazard of limitation upon its freedom exists when it accepts any kind of assistance, whether private or public.

The problem of the church, then, is to weigh this hazard against the opportunity to increase its capabilities for meeting human need in an expanding society. When, and if, the church accepts such aid (in this case federal aid) it must be prepared to face several stern eventualities:

a. The possible termination of such aid because of change in governmental policy;

b. The possible intensification of restrictions or limitations through change in governmental policy;

c. The possibility that the church, by accepting such aid, may dilute or compromise the distinctive quality of its witness;

d. The possibility that, by accepting such aid, the church defines its interpretation of the separation principle and thereby conditions its position on the application of this principle to other forms of aid.

The significance of this document for The American Lutheran Church is to remind its divisions, boards, and members that the liberty of the Christian faith always requires them to be under the tension of decision. Further, this document seeks to state the alternatives so that they may make their choices in full knowledge of both the hazards and the opportunities. Then, whether as divisions, boards, or individual members of the church, they will be able to act with the sense of enlightened Christian responsibility.

Two Types of Aid

We distinguish between two types of federal aid which affect the institutions of the church. One is a grant or a loan directly to a person. The other is a grant or a loan to an institution, whether directly or indirectly. Although both types of aid may involve problems of the relation of church and state, and the application of the distinction between the two types of aid may be difficult, nevertheless the two are unlike in their motivation and should be viewed differently.

Aids to Persons

Federal grants or loans to persons we see as an investment in people and an exercise of the general welfare powers of the Congress. Examples are higher educational benefits for veterans, scholarships and fellowships for superior students, old-age assistance grants, and programs for the training and rehabilitation of handicapped persons. Such programs are based on citizenship, residence, need, special service, or unusual ability of persons. Obviously, these programs must be administered under carefully prescribed policies and procedures without political favoritism, and without discrimination as to race, religion, or national origin.

Church institutions have every right and freedom to serve, and to receive payment from, persons benefitting from such federal assistance. Indeed, to refuse to serve such persons would be an abdication of the church's responsibility. However, such aid, even though lawful, should not be accepted to the extent that its curtailment or elimination would jeopardize the existence of the institution. Nor should such aid be allowed to become so major a factor as to compromise or to subvert the religious character of the institution.

Aids to Institutions

We regard federal loans or grants to church-owned or church-related colleges, hospitals, nursing homes, and homes for older people, whether for capital investment or for normal operations, as presenting greater complications for both church and state than do direct aids to persons.

We recognize, nevertheless, that federal funds have been appropriated and currently are available for colleges, hospitals, nursing homes, and homes for older people. We recognize, too, that institutions of The American Lutheran Church have accepted such funds for expansion of their program and facilities. On the one hand, we feel that the acceptance of governmental loans or grants by institutions of the church may jeopardize their freedom to carry out their distinctive religious functions. On the other hand, we would protest were church-owned and church-related institutions excluded by legislation from federal programs designed to aid colleges, hospitals and nursing homes, and homes for older people. In each of these fields we believe that church agencies are contributing greatly to the general welfare. We insist that they should be eligible to participate in any program of governmental assistance in these areas. Whether they do so or not should be their own choice.

Conditions Under Which Aid Is Accepted

The church cannot by general directives determine the administrative decisions that boards and institutions must make in dealing with specific situations. But, since basic policies affecting the entire church are involved, the following general considerations are advanced as guideposts to boards and institutions in dealing with the matters within their competence.

a. Controls necessarily accompany assistance in any form from any branch of the government. Such control may be explicit in the terms of the grant or the underlying legislation, or it may arise by operation of law since the acceptance of aid may lead to the characterization of the institution as a quasi-governmental agency. Before accepting any such federal aid the church institution must satisfy itself that its essential character, institutional integrity, and freedom to carry out its objectives will not be jeopardized.

b. The church institution must also reckon with the possibility that dependence upon the government through continued acceptance of assistance will ultimately not only lessen its reliance upon the church and private donors but also subject its future operations to the hazards involved in withdrawal of governmental aid.

c. In general, less difficulty in terms of church-state relations is presented when an institution accepts a governmental loan as contrasted with an outright grant. In the case of a loan the institution tenders a specific *quid pro quo*, namely the promise to repay the principal with interest, and when the institution meets the conditions of a loan faithfully and promptly, it completes its obligations except for conditions which may continue as a result of express terms of the contract. Before any institution of the church accepts the offer of a governmental loan, however, it must have every reasonable assurance that it is capable of meeting the financial terms of the contract and any other obligations imposed, without jeopardizing its normal program, plans, and operations.

d. It is possible also that in the case of an outright grant the institution may undertake certain obligations which will terminate at a fixed time. The greater peril to an institution lies in acceptance of outright grants which are not identified with specific services for a limited period but which involve continuing obligations of a public character that may have the effect of impressing the institution with the status of a quasi-governmental agency.

e. A distinction should be observed between nonrecurring loans or grants for capital purposes and annually recurring subsidies to support the institution's operating budget. In general, institutions should avoid recurring subsidies designed to aid the institution in its overall operations. Reliance on such subsidies presents the greatest threat to the institution's continued independence and freedom.

f. It is appropriate for our institutions to enter into contracts for specific services, projects, or programs, but these should not serve to divert the institution from its basic program. Neither should they be permitted to distort or significantly to unbalance the institutional program and objectives.

Extension into Other Spheres

In view of other, continuing, problems in the field of church-state relations, particularly involving prayer and Scripture reading in the public schools, observance of religious holidays, tax exemption for churches, and the like, it is herewith resolved that The American Lutheran Church in Convention Assembled request the Commission on Research and Social Action to prepare study documents for discussion throughout the church and for possible consideration at a subsequent convention of the Church.

C. RELIGIOUS PRACTICES AND THE GOVERNMENT

Prayer in the Public Schools

President Fredrik A. Schiotz in his report to the 1964 Convention referred to the widespread concern about the issue of prayer in the public schools. He attached a statement prepared at his request by Dr. Paul G. Kauper, an ALC member and professor of constitutional law at the University of Michigan. The 1964 Convention adopted the following resolution:

VOTED by the Second General Convention, The American Lutheran Church, October 26, 1964 (GC64.26.118) to adopt the following resolution:

WHEREAS, The president of the church in his message has called attention to the deep concern among our people regarding the Supreme Court decision on prayer in the public schools; and

WHEREAS, There are attempts from many sources to achieve changes via legislative process and constitutional amendment; and

WHEREAS, The president of the church has indicated the desirability of guidance by the church for its people; and

WHEREAS, Dr. Paul Kauper, a professor of constitutional law, has prepared a statement at the request of the president of the church (Report of the President, Exhibit A, pages 89 and 90); therefore be it

Resolved, that this convention commends the president of The American Lutheran Church for his concern relative to the Supreme Court decision regarding prayer in the public schools and the events following the decision; and be it further

Resolved, That the statement by Professor Kauper concerning proposals to amend the United States Constitution to give constitutional sanction to certain types of religious practices in public institutions be commended as a carefully reasoned document for study by the members of The American Lutheran Church.

Proposals are now pending before the Congress of the United States to amend the Constitution in order to give constitutional sanction to certain types of religious practices in public institutions and in the public life. Some of these proposals are directed only to the matter of prayer and Bible reading in the public schools and are designed to overcome the effect of the Supreme Court's decisions dealing with these practices. Others go further and would give constitutional sanction also to references to God and to expressions of belief in God in public ceremonies, in public documents and on the coins or obligations of the United States.

We believe that it would be unwise for the Congress to give its approval to any such amendment. Without attempting to pass judgment on the soundness of the Supreme Court's decisions in declaring officially prescribed prayer and Bible reading practices to constitute an establishment of religion in violation of the First and Fourteenth Amendments to the Constitution, we do recognize that such practices are essentially ritualistic in character, that any form of religious practice opens the way for sectarian intrusion into the public school program, that such practices offend minority groups, and that in the end religion suffers and religious liberty in its fullness is threatened when government uses the power of its laws and the public school program to prescribe an official faith. Devotional exercises for the cultivation and nurture of religious faith belong in the home and the church.

Insofar as some of these proposed amendments are directed to the further purpose of validating references to God on public occasions, and in public ceremonies, proclamations, and documents, they are unnecessary since neither the holdings nor the chief opinions in the cases decided by the Supreme Court support the view that the Constitution outlaws reference to God and to expression of belief and dependence upon him whether it be in the public school or on various public occasions. Moreover, any attempt to deal with these matters by constitutional amendment creates problems and difficulties of draftsmanship and may open the door to practices which encroach upon freedom of belief and conscience.

The Constitution as the basic law of the land should not be amended, particularly in the vital and sensitive areas of religious liberty and of church-state relations, except to achieve some great and compelling public purpose or need. For the reasons stated above, we believe that it would be a step in the wrong direction to amend the Constitution in order to achieve the purposes of the proposals now pending before Congress.

This expression of our disapproval of these proposals for constitutional amendment does not mean that we disapprove of reference to God and to belief in and dependence upon him as found in various aspects of our public life. On the contrary, we believe that these are appropriate practices, not because they contribute to the vitality of the nation's religious life, but because they are a legitimate expression of our religious heritage. Indeed, to say that the Constitution requires the deletion in the public life of all such references rooted in the history and life of our people is to interpret the Constitution as manifesting hostility to religion. It is important also that our public schools recognize the relevance of religion and afford opportunity for study of the Bible and of religion as essential to the purposes of public education.

The Supreme Court's decisions do not outlaw prayer and study of the Bible in the public schools. They prohibit only officially prescribed religious exercises calling for corporate participation. Unfortunately, the Supreme Court's decisions have been relied upon in some instances to furnish pretext and license for the use of the public school classroom both to discredit religion and to deny opportunity for the voluntary expressions by students of their faith. This is a gross distortion of the Supreme Court's decisions. The Constitution assures the free exercise of religion. The schools must see to it that this freedom is fully respected.

Sunday Closing Laws

1964 Convention action: WHEREAS, Laws regulating Sunday business activities affect not only the church but also business, family, recreation, and community life; and

WHEREAS, The American Lutheran Church is interested in the genuine well-being of all persons in every community; therefore be it

Resolved, That The American Lutheran Church commend to its members the following statement for their consideration in deciding their own positions on Sunday closing laws.

Sunday closing laws often become an issue which divides a community. Even religious people often are sharply divided on the question of whether or not to support Sunday closing laws.

Religious issues of course are involved in laws which restrict on Sundays those activities permitted on other days of the week. At stake are freedom of conscience and of justice. Laws which compel Sunday closing discriminate against those whose religion requires them to observe Saturday as their day of rest and worship. Just so, to be required to work on Sunday violates the conscience of many a devout Christian.

One thing is certain. Churches do not need Sunday closing laws in order to protect themselves. Such laws even may harm the churches by leaving the false impression that Christianity is a religion of rules and restrictions, that it opposes joy and happiness in this life, and that it is hypocritical in asking protection for its own holy day under the guise of "a community day of rest."

The Supreme Court of the United States, in accepting the legality of Sunday closing laws, stated the case for "a community day of rest" in these words:

However, the State's purpose is not merely to provide a one-day-in-seven work stoppage. In addition to this, the State seeks to set one day apart from all others as a day of rest, repose, recreation and tranquility— a day which all members of the family and community have the opportunity to spend and enjoy together, a day in which there exists relative quiet and disassociation from the everyday intensity of commercial activities, a day in which people may visit friends and relatives who are not available during working days.

For Christians Sunday indeed is a day set apart. It is the day hallowed by the Lord's resurrection. It is the day for assembling with fellow believers for study, worship, and praise. It is the "change of pace" day for setting aside all but the necessities in favor of those self-chosen activities that bring happiness, satisfaction, contentment, rest, and relaxation. Christians know that a community whose people neglect to hear the preaching of God's word or to learn its message for their lives is scarcely likely to be one where "mercy and truth are met together; righteousness and peace have kissed each other" (Ps. 85:10).

As Lutherans following Luther's explanation of the Third Commandment, we emphasize attitudes toward God's Word above attitudes toward his day. We view Sunday closing laws in terms of their effects upon the physical, mental, moral, and spiritual well-being of persons. Thus we remain faithful to our Lord's teaching, "The sabbath was made for man, not man for the sabbath" (Mark 2:27). We practice St. Paul's counsel, "Let no one pass judgment on you in questions of food and drink or with regard to a festival or a new moon or a sabbath" (Col. 2:16). We believe, nevertheless, that every community needs one day in seven for "rest, repose, recreation, and tranquility" *as well as* for the opportunity it gives for associating with fellow-believers in study, worship, and praise of the eternal God.

We would be naive if we did not recognize that Sunday closing laws involve not only religious but also economic elements. Typically underlying the agitation to ban Sunday sales of various lines of merchandise is economic competition, of discount houses with old-line stores, of suburban shopping centers with downtown merchants, of independents with the chains.

Both sides try to hide the economic issue behind moral arguments. One pleads to save Sundays for families or to keep one day free from normal week-day activities. The other stresses the case for freedom of personal choice, for families to shop together, and the impossibility of confining to six days the needs of a complex, mobile, interdependent society.

We urge that the issue be settled not primarily by law and the force of government but rather by voluntary agreement worked out in each community on the basis of its own needs and experience. We suggest that members of our own congregations buy only necessities on Sunday. They may prefer to patronize those stores which maintain the community pattern of informal, voluntary controls. Not wanting to impose our views on others, we ask that "every one be fully convinced in his own mind" (Rom. 14:5) and act accordingly.

Religious Faith and Political Candidates

The Church Council in 1961 approved for release a statement "Religious Faith as a Factor in American Elections," recommended by the Commission on Research and Social Action, based on similar statements approved in 1960 by the National Lutheran Council and the former American Lutheran Church.

The religious affiliation of a candidate for political office is a valid concern of the voter, but in a democratic order a candidate ought not to be supported or opposed merely on the grounds of his religious affiliation without regard to his record or to his other qualifications.

Unless we are prepared to grant that religion, and, in particular, the Christian faith, is irrelevant to public life in the United States—a proposition which would hardly stand the test of objective examination—it will have to be admitted that the religious faith of any person will influence his private and public conduct to some extent. It is regrettable that the effort is sometimes made to disclaim completely all relevancy of religious convictions to political life. Such disclaimers are a danger sign since they reveal that the "image" of the church in the American mind is such as to make religion essentially irrelevant in those areas where the important decisions of our times are made.

The conduct of public affairs is subject to a multitude of pressures. Since even private conduct, where these pressures are far less complex, is rarely determined exclusively by a person's loyalty to a religious denomination, it is naive to assume that a public officer's conduct of his public office would be exclusively determined by such religious loyalties. Obviously people of varying religious loyalties are constantly required to compromise these loyalties in order to avoid a breakdown in our pluralistic society. There is a great deal of difference between theoretical claims of absolute loyalty which a religious community may be prepared to make and the actual loyalty which it can command. This appears to be true of all religious groups though in varying degrees.

The fitness of a candidate for public office depends upon many qualifications. Such personal qualities as integrity, courage,wisdom, and understanding are essential for a candidate to deserve the support of church people. The past record of the candidate is a legitimate basis for evaluating his future performance. Although a basic change may not be impossible, it would be unwise to anticipate a fundamental reversal of an established pattern as a result of an election. The record of a candidate's party and the avowed policies of his supporters also must be taken into account. Among all these considerations the candidate's religious affiliation is one factor.

It is regrettable that some church people begin to show concern about the qualifications of candidates only when high federal office is involved, neglecting state and local elections and primaries which often are just as important as national elections in deciding policies and leadership in our representative form of government.

To reiterate: the religious affiliation of a candidate for any office is a valid concern of the voter. But it has to be balanced against all the qualifications of this candidate and other candidates, and should not be taken out of the context of the total political situation in which the voter has to make his decision.

D. AREAS OF INSTITUTIONAL ADAPTATION

Saturday/Sunday Voting

In response to a proposal to hold national elections for president, vice-president, and members of Congress on the first Saturday and Sunday in November, the Church Council in 1963 "voted not to approve the proposal to hold election for president and vice-president and members of Congress on two days, Saturday and Sunday."

Religious Census

The Church Council in 1963 "voted to request Congress to make possible, through legislation, a religious census in 1966."

Social Security Coverage for Clergy

The 1966 Convention received the following recommendation from the Board of Pensions:

Resolved, That the Board of Pensions recommend that The American Lutheran Church go on record as favoring the coverage of ministers under Social Security under the following conditions:

1. That the coverage be continued on the self-employed basis so as to preserve the fundamental principle of the separation of church and state.

2. That the coverage of ministers be made mandatory with the right preserved to an individual minister to elect out of Social Security if he has conscientious objections to such coverage.

The Joint Council recommended for adoption the following alternate proposal:

To recommend to the General Convention that The American Lutheran Church go on record as favoring an amendment of the Social Security Act by Congress, so that ministers would be covered under Social Security subject to the following conditions:

1. That the coverage be continued on the self-employed basis so as to preserve the fundamental principle of the separation of Church and State;

2. That the coverage of ministers be made mandatory.

Having considered these and alternate proposals from the floor, the 1966 Convention adopted the following:

That The American Lutheran Church go on record as favoring Social Security as it affects ministers, only as the law is now written.

It is interesting to note that the amendments subsequently enacted by the Congress coincided with the recommendation of the Board of Pensions.

Military Exemption for Divinity Students

The Church Council in 1968 adopted the following statement "On Exemption from Military Service for Divinity Students:"

We recognize that there is no basis in the Scriptures or in the Confessions of the church to separate the clergy or ministerial students from other Christians in the responsibility a citizen may have to serve in the armed forces of his country.

We recognize, further, that in accepting exemption from such service, pastors may indeed as a class isolate themselves from experiences, if not from responsibilities, which their parishioners have had and thus diminish the effectiveness of their ministries.

On the other hand, the decision to exempt divinity students from such service is one made by the government and not by the churches. This law of the land is prompted by a strong tradition in our democracy that the welfare of our people and society, in war as in peace, depends in great measure on the spiritual ministry which the church alone provides, and that, if congregations should suffer a serious shortage of pastors, the very fabric of our national life would be in jeopardy.

Nevertheless, if a man feels conscientiously compelled to enter military service, he is free to do so even under the present system. A pastor or student may volunteer or refuse to accept exemption. But, on the other hand again, it would seem unwise for The American Lutheran Church to take action to deny its members the right to accept the judgment of the government and to prevent from enrolling in its seminaries young men who may otherwise be eligible for military service.

Revision of Income Tax Laws

The Church Council in 1963 "adopted the following resolution regarding Proposed Revision of Income Tax Laws."

WHEREAS, Suggestions have been made to the Congress of the United States concerning certain alterations in the income tax laws, including the specific suggestion that expenditures presently deductible from taxable income, including contributions to religious and charitable bodies, be deductible only to the extent that such expenditures exceed five percent of the taxpayer's adjusted gross income; and

WHEREAS, These suggestions are of significance to the financial program of the church; and

WHEREAS, Members of congregations of the church have requested guidance concerning any action which might be taken with regard to these suggested tax law amendments; therefore be it

Resolved, That the Church Council express the following opinion:

That offering made by a member of the church should be a response to the love of Christ, an expression of the desire to implement the work of the kingdom, and an attempt to comply with the instructions given to us in Scripture. Such giving should not be motivated by a desire to minimize tax obligations nor in any sense a substitute for the fair response of the Christian to the financial demands of his government.

There is, however, valid basis to question the wisdom of a tax law amendment which would limit the deductibility of donations to religious and charitable programs as deductions. The citizen may properly ask if there are not social and spiritual benefits for the entire nation which result when individuals willingly accept the responsibility of providing certain services, which values are diminished or lost when the same or similar services are provided through tax sources.

Benevolent contributions are essentially different in nature from the other categories of tax-deductible expenses. They are at the giver's discretion; they are not self-serving in character but represent the exercise of altruism; they constitute a constructive act of enlightened citizenship. It would be unfortunate to have religious and charitable contributions lumped together with other deductions in a move to "close tax loopholes," giving the false impression that benevolent giving is considered in this light. It might be a sounder public policy, if a five percent floor is to be applied to deductible expenses, to remove the "Contributions" category from this new provision. This would be consonant with the historic recognition on the part of the federal government of the social value of voluntary benevolent giving.

It is indeed possible that the existing deduction privilege may be abused by many people. The church must be cautious that it does not unwittingly facilitate, or even appear to facilitate, evasions of proper tax liability. Congregations of the church should re-examine their accounting procedures to be certain that adequate and accurate records are kept and furnished to all members.

Tax Exemption

On recommendation of the Board of Trustees, the 1964 Convention adopted a resolution "to draw to the attention of all congregations and institutions in the United States that (1) a condition of the Internal Revenue Service in the application of the blanket exemption is that all exempt agencies declare in their Articles of Incorporation that in the event of disbandonment, the property of the congregation or institution will revert to another tax exempt agency; (2) the exemption refers only to such income as is derived from the performance of the purposes for which the congregation or institution is incorporated."

E. PROPOSALS FOR FEDERAL ACTION

Home Rule for the District of Columbia

The Church Council, acting in 1967 on recommendation of the Commission on Research and Social Action, approved the following statement on "Home Rule for the District of Columbia" "for circulation and study in the congregations of The American Lutheran Church and for such action as members may wish to take."

Background

The Eastern District Convention in 1966 adopted a resolution going "on record as recognizing that the right of self-government and the election of officials charged with local affairs should be immediately extended to the residents of the District of Columbia." It further requested a General Convention "resolution supporting home rule for the district . . . and to inform the representatives in Congress of this action."

The 1966 General Convention referred this Memorial from the Eastern District to the Commission on Research and Social Action "for its examination and the formulation of a statement covering the issues, this statement to be made available to the Church Council or its Executive Committee at an early date for such action as may be indicated."

The Issue

To cut to the heart of the issue is difficult. To identify the grounds on which the ALC should speak, and the counsel it should voice, is even more difficult. For, the issue has a tangible history, it is tangled in the webs of racism, and it revolves around a constitutional question. The Constitution (Article I, Section 8) declares that the Congress shall have power:

"17. To exercise exclusive legislation in all cases whatsoever over such district (not exceeding ten miles square) as may, by cession of particular States and the acceptance of Congress, become the seat of Government of the United States, and to exercise like authority over all places purchased by the consent of the Legislature of the State in which the same shall be, for the erection of forts, magazines, arsenals, dockyards, and other needful buildings."

Washington, D.C., is not just another city. It is the "seat of government," the capital city, of the United States. The Constitution makes plain that all real estate owned and used for federal governmental purposes must be under the exclusive authority of the Congress. In no cases shall federal government properties, operations, or processes be subject to state or local authority or legislation. The federal government must remain free to manage its own affairs and control its own facilities. It must be free from even the possibility of harassment, intimidation, or threats of any other governmental unit. It must remain immune from taxation and the subservience which subjection to taxation implies.

The Need for Self-Government

"Home Rule" for the District could only be limited or conditional. Congress cannot grant to the District any powers which would pose threats or hazards to the free and responsible operations of the federal government. Yet Congress can delegate certain powers of self-government to residents of Washington, D.C., as it did from 1802 until 1874.

People living within the District require, after all, the usual array of basic governmental services—schools, libraries, police and fire protection, courts, licensing and record-keeping, correctional institutions, hospitals, sanitation, welfare, recreation, streets and highways, and construction and maintenance of public buildings, etc. Taxes are levied upon and paid by the residents to provide these services.

The residents have no voice, however, either in levying these taxes, deciding how the revenues shall be allocated, or shaping the policies within which these basic local government services are rendered. Rather, Congress governs the District through its House and Senate committees on the District of Columbia and on Appropriations. Limited powers are delegated to a three-man Board of Commissioners (replaced by a single Commissioner and a nine-man Council in a reorganization move proposed by President Johnson, effective August 11, 1967), and to a series of federal agencies, authorities, boards, and officers. Not one of these, however, is chosen by or answerable to the residents of the District.

Washington, D.C., in effect is a "company town," run by the biggest property owner and largest employer, the United States Government. Its board of directors, the Congress, allows itself to decide local issues which should be resolved by a city council or state legislature directly responsive to the immediately concerned constituency.

Possibilities for Limited Home Rule

We believe that fairness and justice argue that residents of the District be granted limited powers of self-government. We believe that the quality of civic life, civic pride, and responsible interest in civic affairs in Washington, D.C., would be significantly improved were residents of the District delegated powers to choose their own local officials, to develop their own local governmental policies, and to act on their convictions as to the quality of the basic services which they are receiving. We believe that this course builds wholesomely upon man's self-interest, his resentment against paternalism, and his capacity to derive satisfaction from a trust successfully handled.

In keeping with the unique character of Washington as the nation's capital city, certain safeguards must be provided to assure a representative government accountable to the Congress. We cite these:

1. Governmental structures must recognize that Washington, D.C., functions as both a city and a state so far as programs of federal grants-in-aid are concerned:

2. Only genuine residents, not those in Washington for a limited term of governmental service nor those who retain legal residence in another state, should be permitted to vote or hold District office;

3. Congress must pledge itself to make payments to the District in lieu of taxes, perhaps in some fixed ratio to the taxes raised under self-government. Without some such Congressional pledge of financial support "home rule" is doomed to failure, for the District cannot operate on the tax base open to it.

The Factor of Racism

Home rule for Washington may be unwise or difficult on constitutional or other practical grounds. To deny the possibility of home rule solely on racial considerations is an insult to our Negro neighbors. We anticipate with some satisfaction the possibility that many of the locally elected political leaders of Washington would be Negro. We are confident that in ability and performance they will compare favorably with public officials in other American cities and states.

Our Conclusion

As a Commission on Research and Social Action we encourage members of The American Lutheran Church to express their views on Home Rule for the District of Columbia to their respective Representatives and Senators. Voices from "back home" can be highly influential.

For our part we believe that enlightened statesmanship argues that the Congress should delegate to residents of the District controlled powers of self-government in local affairs. In so doing the Congress must pledge itself to pay, in lieu of taxes, a fair share of the revenues the District requires to meet the demands expected of it as the nation's capital city. Washington, D.C., is a city-state which belongs not only to its residents. It belongs to all of the people of the United States. Every American wishes to take pride in his capital city as a symbol of that which he believes represents the best of America and its way of life.

Human Rights Conventions

The Church Council, acting in 1967 on recommendation of the Commission on Research and Social Action, approved the following statement on "U.S. Ratification of Human Rights Conventions" "for transmission to the congregations of The American Lutheran Church for study."

The United States prides itself on its dedication to life, liberty, and the pursuit of happiness. It declares its concern for human rights, civil liberties, and protection of the person against exploitation by government. The United States has played an influential role in shaping declarations of human rights intended to represent the universal aspirations of mankind.

Yet, the United States has not adopted any of the United Nations-sponsored conventions, covenants, or treaties that seek to give legal standing to the broad declarations. President Truman proposed that the Senate approve the Convention on Genocide. President Kennedy proposed approval of Conventions on the Political Rights of Women, on Abolition of Forced Labor, and a Supplemental Convention on Slavery. President Johnson has recommended approval of these Human Rights conventions.

Critics of U.S. inaction hold that the U.S. sacrifices its moral leadership for human rights and for constructive influence in developing a solid body of international law. These rights already are assured to Americans by the Bill of Rights. They should be made the birthright of every human being, say the sponsors of U.S. ratification of the Conventions. Otherwise, the younger nations will not make serious effort to incorporate these protections into their own constitutions.

Prime objections to ratification seem to be legal or constitutional rather than moral. The "Connally Reservation" of 1946 and the "Bricker Amendment" controversy of the mid-1950s symbolized the doubts of many Americans on how much power it is wise to transfer to an international organization and whether treaties and executive agreements may in effect become instruments for amending the domestic constitution. It was feared that the Conventions would become a means whereby other nations could involve themselves in the domestic affairs of the U.S. It also was stated that the objectives sought in the four Conventions are matters of state rather than federal legislation, so could not be enforced by the federal government. Critics argue further than "human rights" are not a proper area for treaty making between nations.

In light of intensely held views favoring or opposing U.S. ratification of the U.N.-sponsored Conventions on human rights a brief summary of each of four Conventions seems indicated:

I. Genocide is made a crime under international law, and parties to the Convention agree to punish guilty persons, so determined under domestic courts or international panel. Five acts, "if accompanied by intent to destroy, in whole or part, a national, ethnical, racial, or religious group," are defined as genocide: "(a) killing members of the group; (b) causing serious bodily or mental harm to members of the group; (c) deliberately inflicting on the group conditions of life calculated to bring about its physical destruction in whole or in part; (d) imposing measures intended to prevent births within the group; and (e) forcibly transferring children of the group to another."

II. Political Rights of Women provides that, on equal terms with men and without discrimination, women shall: *first*, be entitled to vote in all elections; *second*, be eligible for election to all publicly elected bodies established by national law; and *third*, be entitled to hold public office and exercise all public functions established by national law.

III. Supplemental Convention on Slavery elaborating a 1926 Convention to which the U.S. is a party, requires all practicable and necessary measures to bring about as soon as possible the complete abolition of such practices as debt bondage, serfdom, involuntary marriage, or transfer of women for payment, transfer of widows as inherited property, and exploitation of children. It also names participation in the slave trade and the marking or branding of slaves or persons of servile status as criminal offenses.

IV. Abolition of Forced Labor requires signatory members to suppress and not to make use of any form of forced or compulsory labor "(a) as a means of political coercion or education or as a punishment for holding or expressing political views or views ideologically opposed to the established political, social or economic system; (b) as a method of mobilizing and using labour for purpose of economic development; (c) as a means of labour discipline; (d) as a punishment for having participated in strikes; (e) as a means of racial, social, national, or religious discrimination."

The American Lutheran Church is in full agreement with the intent and objectives these Conventions seek to realize. Yet it is fully aware that the language in its very brevity may become inaccurate, vague, or fuzzy. Each lends itself to the possibility of strained interpretations or hypocritical invoking of the sanctions behind the Conventions.

Will the Iron Curtain countries accuse the U.S. of genocide because it is "causing serious bodily or mental harm" to Negroes, or the Viet Cong? Who will intervene to insure that Iron Curtain countries give full religious freedom to Jews, Moslems, and Christians? Must women be accorded the right to serve on a police force or in the military? Is prison labor forbidden? What country cannot find a person it considers notorious on other counts to have been guilty of breaking some civil law, whether income tax evasion or currency manipulation? Who will judge and enforce the competing claims and counter-claims, and by what standards?

These and other possible questions indeed may cause anxiety. Nevertheless, the Church Council commends to the members of the ALC the following resolution, adapted from one referred in January 1966 by the Executive Committee of the National Lutheran Council to the church bodies participating in the Council:

WHEREAS, Four Conventions adopted by the United Nations and ratified by many other nations have been submitted for ratification by the United States Senate; and

WHEREAS, Representatives of the United States government took an influential role in the drafting of these Conventions; and

WHEREAS, These Conventions deal with such important issues in the area of human rights as the prevention and punishment of genocide, practices akin to slavery, forced labor, and the guarantee of political rights of women; and

WHEREAS, It is fitting that the United States should exercise moral leadership in promoting the respect for and observance of human rights both in its domestic life and in the development of international law; and

WHEREAS, Christians, in keeping with their understanding of man as a person created in the image of God, have a special responsibility to foster the recognition of human dignity, responsibility, and free choice in the structures of society; therefore be it

Resolved, That members of The American Lutheran Church be encouraged to inform themselves on these Conventions, their text and intentions, the values which are at stake, and measures necessary to make them effective in our federal system, and to share the results of their informed study with their respective senators.

IV

War and Conscience

A. A BASIC STANCE

The 1964 Convention was faced with a statement on "Issues of War and Peace," submitted by the Commission on Research and Social Action. That Convention referred the statement back to the Commission for further study, specifying five areas for attention, requested widespread study and discussion of the redraft at conference and district conventions in 1964-65, and anticipated action on the revised statement in 1966. The Commission submitted to the 1966 Convention a new draft, "War, Peace, and Freedom." Action by the 1966 Convention adopted the following resolution.

WHEREAS, A predecessor statement was referred back to the Commission on Research and Social Action by the 1964 General Convention with suggestions for revision; and

WHEREAS, The proposals for revision have been considered and incorporated into the present draft; and

WHEREAS, Generally favorable comments have been expressed on the current draft since its circulation in the spring and early summer of 1965; therefore be it

Resolved, That The American Lutheran Church adopt the following statement as expressing its views on the sensitive issues of war and peace as a guide to its members and as a contribution to public discussion.

The Issues in Tension

As perhaps never before in human history, men fear and dread war. They fear that through the weapons of total warfare now available, man will destroy himself, his civilization, and this present world. In contrast, the promises of peace, of a social order subject to man's control, of a world without war hold a strong appeal.

War is war, even though it may not be total war, nor even declared war. It may be a limited military action, waged within a relatively small geographic area, involving comparatively few combatants. Methods of warfare include guerrilla action, blockade, infiltration, subversion, and other means of undermining a people's will or capacity to resist. War thus may include not only military action but also economic and psychological weapons.

The price of freedom may be so high as to require war. Peace, freedom, and security come dear. It is possible that a nation and its people cannot have peace, security, and freedom. Under some circumstances their only alternatives may be either the peace of surrender to tyranny and totalitarianism or the security and freedom bought by risking and engaging in war.

To people caught in the tensions between war and peace, totalitarianism and freedom, life and death, the Church of Jesus Christ needs to speak relevant counsel. Members of The American Lutheran Church ought to be vocal in helping to clarify and to shape public policy on issues of war, peace, and the demands of responsible freedom. The Commission on Research and Social Action offers the results of its discussions as a stimulus to widespread thinking and discussion of these issues within The American Lutheran Church, to be carried by the members into the discussions within the body politic.

The Paradox of War

War is an evil scourge, which like famine and pestilence brings destruction to mankind. War denies God's central commandment of love (Matt. 22:37-40). War is a consequence of a world estranged from God, a fruit of sinful man's passions. (See James 4:1.) Man's sinfulness shows in such traits as pride, arrogance, greed, lust for power, divisiveness, hate, bigotry, self-righteousness, and idolatry, including an unquestioning devotion to the goals and the supremacy of his own nation. These, in the complex intermingling of causes and effects and in the involved workings of man's reason and his madness, are what lead to war.

God's plan and purpose for man do not require war. When man's disobedience brings war, God can transform it into a chastening of sinful, rebellious men and nations that deny his Lordship and defy his demands for justice and mercy. God may turn war's waste of life, energy, and resources into a reminder of the folly of trusting in material things. God's use of pagan nations to rebuke the idolatry and wickedness of Israel and Judah testifies to his judgment through war.

Although war indeed may result in scientific advance and material progress, and may bring out some of the noblest qualities in the human spirit as men are moved to deny self for the well-being of others, war also gives demonic satisfaction to some of the basest elements in humanity. Cruelties and injustice are inflicted; greed and avarice run rampant; lust and license are made to appear as virtues; internal enemies can be silenced; critics are ridiculed; and power-mad men ruthlessly impose their wills upon others. Man's inhumanity to man can take its most extreme forms in war.

The inhumanity of war ought not be measured solely by the destructive power of the weapons used. The madness which moved men to throw stones, hurl spears, or shoot arrows is little different in quality from the cold, impersonal technology which unleashes the nuclear, chemical, or biological weapons man now has at hand. Those killed are just as dead, probably having died more quickly under the latter than under the earlier weaponry. While wars of massive destructiveness are not new in human experience man now seems to have it within his power through total war to bring this world to an end.

In every age men and nations have sought to renounce war as a defensible instrument of national policy. To their dismay they often found that the more loudly they spoke their love for peace and their hatred for war, the more certainly they became involved in wars of defense against an aggressor who misjudged their will to resist his dominance. It appears that war is least likely to erupt when the probable contestants are equally weak and equally incapable of waging war, equally strong and balanced and thus equally sure that they could not win the contest, or equally sure that the opponent possesses not only military power but also the will to use it.

The "Just War" Question

War can be seen as an emergency use of temporal power exercised by the civil rulers, an extension of the authority they derive from God to maintain order and justice (Rom. 13:1-4). As Creator and Preserver, God has decreed laws binding upon all men, obedience to which is essential for civic righteousness. (See Ps. 19:7-11; Prov. 14:34; Matt. 22:17-21.) God has conferred a measure of his authority upon duly-constituted government in order to promote, foster, and protect justice, morality, equity, peace, order, and respect for inalienable human rights (Ps. 82, Rom. 13, Titus 3). Government must restrain, if need be by force, those who would deprive human beings of these divine blessings.

The very readiness to risk war and the very willingness to engage in war may be the only means the nation and its people have for assuring their independence and the preservation of their God-given opportunities and responsibilities. The forces of evil may become so fierce that men will rise in moves of desperation to curb demonic powers. A government may be so tyrannical or despotic that men seek to overthrow it. War may become a means to defend moral and spiritual values cherished more highly than goods or life.

This line of reasoning finds support in Article XVI of the Augsburg Confession, which declares: "Christians may without sin . . . engage in just wars, serve as soldiers. . . ." Christians of that day were ready to judge whether a particular war was a just war on the criteria of whether it (1) seemed to be fought for a just cause, (2) was motivated by a just intent, (3) was waged in accord with the spirit of justice and mercy, and (4) would result in the triumph and reign of justice and mercy for both victor and vanquished. This thinking, which prompted Augsburg XVI, needs to be understood not as justifying war *per se* but as giving criteria by which to evaluate the justice or injustice of a particular war.

The conditions and assumptions which underlay Augsburg's guidance for Christians to "engage in just wars" rarely prevail today. Widely circulated propaganda and managed news cut away the foundation necessary for informed and objective decision-making. Total war wipes out any meaningful distinctions between voluntary enlistment and the draft, between bearing or not bearing arms, between combatants and noncombatants, between the fighting front and the home front, between military objectives and total victory. The decision of whether or not to go to war is a corporate decision made by the political authorities. No citizen can be excused from the massive mobilization of effort which total war demands.

It is the Christian's duty, therefore, as a loyal citizen to obey the demands of his government unless he feels conscience-bound to resist. Not knowing the subtleties of diplomacy and the intricacies of statecraft which brought his nation to the precipice of war, he must trust the soundness of judgment of its leaders. Should he lose confidence in their judgment, their integrity, or the rightness of their course, he must work for changes in his nation's policies, objectives, or leadership. If he is sufficiently convinced that his nation is on a course hostile to God's will. the Christian has the right and the duty to resist. As he does so he knows that he must be willing to accept the consequences, both spiritual and civic. Equally as surely must the person who supports and participates in carrying out the policies of his nation examine his own conscience and the moral consequences of his own action.

Such counsel of obedience to a corporate decision—save only when bound to obey God rather than man—does not deny the evil of war. It is tragic and lamentable when antagonistic nations, in the sinfulness of mankind, are unable to resolve differences they consider fundamental and so turn to war to establish their mastery. War can be understood as a seemingly necessary last resort to which sinful men and nations turn in their desperation. War cannot, however, be called good, righteous, or holy.

Certainly no nation today should be completely autonomous, with unchecked power by force to impose its will upon other peoples. Its claims for the justice of its objectives and the rightness of its actions must be weighed against the higher imperative of God's will for the good of the entire world (John 3:16-21). The "governing authorities" of Rom. 13:1 are not limited to the nation-state as we know it. They include any and all local, national, and international structures effectively exercising governmental powers and which remain faithful to God's purposes for good government.

Christians must weigh the claims of every governing authority for support of the honor, justice, integrity, and rightness of its cause in light of their own understanding of the divine imperative. They must resist the effort of any government to bind or restrict what they believe to be their proper Christian response to God's love for them and for the world.

The Church's Task

The Christian rightly looks to his church for guidance in evaluating the claims and counter-claims for the justice and morality of the cause of the nations approaching the brink or in the throes of war. When men and nations are torn by strife and dissension, leaders of each position invoke high moral and ethical principles to justify their stand. Their conflicts of power and interest produce their need for self-defense, which in turn often becomes self-righteousness. Church leaders therefore need to beware lest they be used to give religious sanction or theological justification to a war which is no more than a naked power struggle for material advantage.

Even so, however, the church through synods, councils, and interchurch assemblies should seek to cut through the barrage of propaganda, smokescreens, and verbiage to discover as best as fallible men can discover where truth, righteousness, justice, and mercy reside. It ought to express its collective prophetic judgment on the morality of the issues of national self-interest at stake, the validity of the objectives the opponents claim, the wisdom of the policies pursued, the possible points on which the conflicting interests honorably can be reconciled, and the probable consequences of the struggle upon such values as justice, freedom, long-range peace, and respect for persons. Members of the church have the right to hear from their spiritual leaders such a reasoned evaluation, interpretation, and judgment as a guide to their own enlightened Christian response to their duties as citizens.

As the universal, all-embracing arm of Jesus Christ, the church should rise above the partisanship of nation, race, or class in offering the gospel of reconciliation. Though pastors and parishioners normally remain loyal to their nation, their higher loyalty is to Jesus Christ and his inclusive body of believers. Churchmen should avoid building walls of hostility toward persons who reside in the land of the enemy, which only deepen and intensify the differences to be resolved. "Love your enemy" is a divine injunction easier to follow before conflict rages than during and after a war.

The church also must minister to those caught in the enmity of war, strife, and dissension. Both those in the armed forces and those on the home front need to hear the comforting, sustaining, interpretive counsel of Jesus Christ to people who find themselves in difficult times. Ministers of Jesus Christ stress the duties and obligations of citizens critically to obey the governing authorities, save only when commanded to sin, to support with vigor such of the nation's goals and objectives which are in harmony with God's purposes, and to pray for an honorable resolution of the conflict, culminating in the triumph of justice and mercy.

The church necessarily shows a deep concern for members of the armed forces and their families. It recognizes how lives are disrupted by the call to military service. Men faced with service on the fighting front, with killing and being killed, need the special spiritual care and counsel of competent chaplains. The church encourages able pastors to enter the chaplaincy ministry and maintains continuing, supportive contacts with them in their special ministry. Pastors and parishioners on the home front remember in their prayers the members of the armed forces. They seek in various specific ways to remind those of their own congregation who are away in military service of the bonds of affection and fellowship which the home congregation feels for the absent brethren.

To men hoping to build a world without war, the church must speak words of encouragement, yet realism. The goal of developing alternate ways of dealing with strife and conflict between nations, short of war, should command the prayers, support, and enthusiastic encouragement of the church. At the same time man cannot be sure that this goal is fully attainable in this present world. Certainly no program of political or international action can be based upon a simple reading of Jesus' words concerning "wars and rumors of wars" (Mark 13:7; also Luke 21:9) or of Isaiah's vision of an era when "nation shall not lift up sword against nation, neither shall they learn war any more" (Isa. 2:4; also Mic. 4:3).

Having a clear view of human sinfulness, which results in jealousy, envy, hostility, and divisiveness, Christians are sure that the seeds of conflict and war never can be totally eliminated from this present world. They dare not, however, take the position that a specific war is inevitable. Rather, they should lend their influence and efforts to work for preventing those struggles and contests in which men and nations exert military power, violence, and force against one another. They should work for justice, harmony, mutual respect and good will, and freedom from violence and civil disturbance which men call peace (Matt. 5:9, Rom. 12:18).

Many a dispute between nations has been settled peaceably, with honor to the adversaries, and with freedom, justice, and equity the fruits of the agreement. Christians strive for an increase in the good will, mutual trust, calm reason, devotion to humanity, and hardheaded realism which will make it easier for nations to resolve their differences by methods short of armed aggression.

A Climate for Better Understanding

Basic to any realistic hope for bringing war under control is a change in men's minds and hearts. People must come to feel that the unity, strength, development, and well-being of mankind are values dearer than racial or national advantage (Gen. 1:27; John 3:16; Acts 17:26). Toward this end it is helpful to stress:

a. The oneness of the human race in creation, sin, and God's offer of salvation through faith in Jesus Christ;

b. The similarities as well as the differences in the hopes, ways of living, and basic social institutions of men, regardless of tongue, flag, color, or faith;

c. The unusual abilities and special gifts which the diversity of men and cultures brings to the richness of human life;

d. The validity of a government being dependent not so much upon its form or structure as upon its ability to govern effectively, fairly, and impartially and upon its willingness to recognize, to respect, and to honor basic human rights.

Various programs seek to put such goals of international person-to-person understanding and good will into action. Current national hostilities ought not be allowed to obstruct programs which promise to relieve actual human need. Each program has hazards to which participants need ever remain alert. Each program ought preferably to be an avenue of genuine two-way contact and communication. Each offers an exciting outlet for action worthy of the energies of self-giving persons. Among such international programs are:

a. Cultural exchange, the sharing with others of features highly esteemed in the sending country and welcomed by the receiving country;

b. People to people visits in the homes as well as to the economic, religious, and civic centers of the host country;

c. Counterpart or twin city ties by which municipal leaders of paired cities exchange ideas on questions of urban life;

d. Study grants and projects, including some opportunity for the student to become a member of a family circle;

e. Voluntary and governmental programs helping people and communities to achieve better agriculture, industry, housing, health, and sanitation;

f. Emergency assistance of food, clothing, and medical supplies to meet human needs, even in hostile lands, when disaster strikes, especially on a church-to-church partnership basis;

g. Sharing in the free flow of ideas and in struggles to win and responsibly to exercise basic human liberties and freedoms.

Along with these civic actions which they can share with any person of good will, members of The American Lutheran Church also can:

a. Manifest in their own lives the positive qualities of peace, patience, kindness, gentleness, and self-control with which the Holy Spirit can empower them;

b. Pray daily and fervently that all men everywhere, especially the rulers of the nations, will come to know and to do God's will in the conduct of public office, and to accept Jesus Christ as their personal Savior;

c. Support with their interest, prayers, personnel, and funds the world-wide missionary program of their church, including its volunteer and short-term service opportunities, by which the gospel of Jesus Christ is brought to every continent;

d. Participate in Lutheran World Relief drives and learn where, how, and with what results the funds and materials are distributed;

e. Inform themselves on the activities and projects of the Lutheran World Federation and share in them as opportunity permits;

f. Cooperate in ecumenical programs seeking to realize the goals of peace and international good will.

As Christians, convinced of the lordship of Jesus Christ, we believe that to the extent that men hear about him, accept him as Lord and Savior, and live in total commitment to his way of love, prospects for peace and freedom thereby brighten. We believe, therefore, that freedom for religious witness and the free exercise of religion are essential for such a better world.

Bringing War Under Control

Neither "peace at any price," nor naive reliance on the words of the enemy, nor allegiance to Utopian goals can bring war under control. Voluntary, governmental, and intergovernmental measures, built upon the foundations of good will and mutual understanding between people, can help. How wise, how prudent, even how realistic or possible a proposed course of action may be, should be subjected to intense discussion and debate.

We urge committed Christians to take part in the arguments seeking the strengths and the pitfalls of such measures for cutting the risk of war as:

a. Cooperation in responsible efforts, both governmental and voluntary, to alleviate material and psychological deprivations suffered by human beings all over the world, which create in them a seedbed for suspicion, hate, and war;

b. Multilateral reduction of armaments to the types and levels necessary to maintain domestic tranquility and order, with effective, verified, reliable checks and controls to insure adherence to arms reduction agreements.

c. An orderly transition whereby excess manpower and materials devoted to armaments can be turned to goods and services yielding a higher quality of personal and community life;

d. International cooperation and control to insure the peaceful uses of outer space;

e. Technical assistance to younger nations in developing their own resources and traditions so that they can take a strong, cooperative, responsible, viable place in the community of nations;

f. Development of a sense of regional and world community through voluntary associations of free nations united by history, values, and goals, and evidenced by mutual cooperation and adherence to covenants which protect the freedoms and liberties of responsible men;

g. Establishment, strengthening, and support of agencies of international conciliation, arbitration, and justice, which seek under law to resolve in honor, equity, and impartiality any major disputes which arise between nations and which possess legitimate power and delegated authority to enforce their decisions;

h. Increased intergovernmental cooperation in cultural, educational, economic, and social spheres to achieve goals of human welfare beyond the capacity of any one nation.

Reaching a Christian Position

The traditional Lutheran doctrine of the "Two Kingdoms" requires that in discussing issues of war and peace we not confuse the roles of church and state. "The gospel cannot legislate for the civil estate." Rather, God seeks to rule through both the civil and the ecclesiastical realms in order to accomplish his gracious purposes and to thwart the evil powers. The church's task is to proclaim the whole counsel of God, tell of his mighty acts, denounce sin and evil, offer his reconciliation, and assist in counteracting the causes of war both in persons and among nations.

As Redeemer and Sanctifier God works through the means of grace, administered by the Church, offering to men the saving truth revealed in Jesus Christ. The faith of the Christian should manifest itself in words and deeds of love, alike in personal piety and in meeting the obligations of his life in community. Through the means of grace the Holy Spirit seeks to guide the believer to the decisions he must make on issues of war, peace, and freedom, as in other civic affairs. God thus would rule in the hearts and lives of his people, who dwell as Christians in both kingdoms.

Pastors in their preaching and teaching bring to their people the counsel of God's word. Members of the priesthood of all believers deserve such help, from pulpit, lectern, and classroom, and from synods, councils, and interchurch assemblies, in thinking through the issues of war and peace and in taking an informed position on them. Above all, people need to act with knowledge, understanding, judgment, and assurance. In their office as citizens they have an obligation to work toward bringing about a world where justice, righteousness, freedom, peace, truth, and love may increase and prevail.

Making the right decision on specific issues is an agonizing task. The Christian gropes for the greater good. He knows that whatever course he chooses he is not entirely free from sin. In the process of reaching his decision he wisely seeks the counsel of his pastor and of trusted fellow Christians. Yet, having decided, he acts boldly and with confidence, knowing that in Jesus Christ his every sinful decision and action is forgiven.

Conscientious Objection

Historically the teaching of the Lutheran church, based on its understanding of the Bible, has been that a Christian as a citizen willingly should assume the duties of citizenship, including the bearing of arms and engaging in "just war."

However, the church recognizes that on the basis of their understanding of the total message of Scripture and the traditions of the early church some of its members arrive at the conviction that they cannot with good conscience bear arms. The American Lutheran Church therefore sustains the individual who reaches this conviction in the necessity of following the dictates of his conscience.

The American Lutheran Church appreciates that government recognizes the demands of conscience and provides alternate channels by which he whose conscience forbids him to bear arms may serve the needs of his country. The American Lutheran Church respectfully asks that the pertinent provisions for alternate service be applied to those of its members whose conscience impels them to refuse the bearing of arms and commends to its members who are conscientious objectors those alternatives for fulfilling the responsibility of citizenship. It recognizes its duty to minister spiritually to the conscientious objector as well as to him who for conscience sake bears arms for his country.

In Conclusion

Christians with contrite and repentant hearts must accept their share of guilt for many of the wars of the Christian era. Often they have felt a numbing complacency that failed to work for peace, that accepted war as inevitable, that harbored the illusion that peace would come without effort once the war was won.

Now we know that humanity can be degraded by war. Inhumanity in any form violates the basic tenets of our faith. Man's welfare can be crippled by warfare. The time has come for all men to seek alternatives to war. Even so, as a means for deterring aggression, maintaining human liberties, and assuring justice war sometimes may become man's last desperate resort to prevent the total victory of evil powers in a sinful, fallen world.

As envoys of Jesus Christ, living in the power of his cross and his forgiveness, we dedicate ourselves anew to his benedictory charge, "Go therefore and make disciples of all nations . . . teaching them to observe all that I have commanded you" (Matt. 28:19, 20). We covet his accolade of "peacemakers," whom he called "sons of God" (Matt. 5:9).

Nonetheless, we are not so desirous of saving our own lives that we surrender to "peace at any price." We recognize with the Apostle Paul (Rom. 12:18) that the possibility of living peaceably with all does not rest entirely with us. Rather, with him we insist "Do not be overcome by evil, but overcome evil with good" (Rom. 12:21).

"O God, the Father in heaven: Grant thy mighty aid to the efforts of men to establish peace among the nations of the world. Give strength of purpose to those who lead; enlighten those who sit in council; and so transform the hearts of men everywhere by thy gracious Gospel, that they may exalt peace above war, service above gain, and righteousness above glory; through Jesus Christ, our Lord. Amen."*

B. CONSCIENTIOUS OBJECTION

The Church Council in 1961 asked the Theological Council "to prepare a statement of policy with regard to conscientious objectors." A progress report was given in 1962 and the Church Council referred the study back to the Theological Council acting jointly with the Commission on Research and Social Action. The Church

---

* From Service Book and Hymnal, Collects and Prayers, "58. For peace," page 226.

Council in 1963 approved the resultant "Statement on Conscientious Objectors." This statement was included in Section H of the draft "Issues of War and Peace," one of the sections singled out as needing further attention. The 1963 Church Council statement on "Conscientious Objectors" is as follows:

The American Lutheran Church recognizes that Christians have differed in the matter of their participation in war.

The teaching of the Lutheran church, based on its understanding of the Bible, has always been that a Christian as a citizen should be willing to assume the duties of citizenship, including the bearing of arms and the engaging in warfare.

However, the Church recognizes that on the basis of certain Bible passages some of its members can arrive at the conviction that they cannot with good conscience bear arms.

The American Lutheran Church respects the conscience of the member who, amid the agony of choices, comes to this conviction and sustains that individual in the necessity of following the dictates of his conscience.

The American Lutheran Church appreciates that enlightened government has taken conscientious objection into account and has wisely provided for alternate service. The American Lutheran Church respectfully asks that the pertinent provisions be applied to those of its members whose conscience impels them to refuse the bearing of arms.

The American Lutheran Church recognizes its duty to minister to the spiritual needs of the conscientious objector as well as of him who for conscience sake will bear arms for his country.

The section on conscientious objection in "War, Peace, and Freedom," adopted in 1966, is the resultant redraft to reflect the church's then current view on this issue.

By 1966 the issue of selective conscientious objection emerged. The following motion was introduced—and rejected—during the discussion of "War, Peace, and Freedom":

WHEREAS, The American Lutheran Church recognizes that some Christians may be as much troubled in conscience regarding participation in a particular war as they may be by participation in war in general; therefore be it

Resolved, That The American Lutheran Church petition the government to redefine conscientious objection to include "selective conscientious objection" and make it possible for those whose conscience forbids them to bear arms in a particular war to be made eligible to participate in the alternate channels of service to the country which are now open to those who conscientiously object to bearing arms in all wars.

In 1968 the Convention received—but referred back to the Commission on Research and Social Action for further study—a proposed statement on Selective Conscientious Objection. One paragraph of that statement was adopted, and is incorporated into paragraph 8 of "National Service and Selective Service Reform."

C. NATIONAL SERVICE AND SELECTIVE SERVICE REFORM

The Commission on Research and Social Action chose to broaden its restudy of selective conscientious objection. It submitted for 1970 Convention consideration a statement on "National Service and Selective Service Reform," which the Convention adopted as a policy statement of The American Lutheran Church in paragraphs 6-8 and as a statement in paragraphs 1-5 "expressing its judgment and corporate conviction as its contribution to the discussions seeking an informed solution to a difficult problem of contemporary life and society."

Service to the nation takes many forms. In a broad sense it includes all endeavors which contribute to the well-being of the country. More specifically it refers to those activities, determined by the Congress to be in the national interest, in which men and women may participate apart from the normal patterns of their occupational training. National service includes social services as well as military activities. Such service usually is for a short period of time and may be on either a voluntary or a mandatory basis. The Peace Corps, VISTA (Volunteers in Service to America), the Teachers' Corps, community action programs, and military duty are examples of national service.

National service accomplishes more than the meeting of critical needs of national defense. It also engages the energies and idealism of men and women in peaceful and constructive pursuits. Among these are teaching, community and agricultural development, health care services, and conservation measures both in this country and abroad. Such social service normally should be on a voluntary basis.

Current public attention is focused upon reform of the Selective Service System. Americans traditionally have regarded military conscription as a measure for times of national crisis. For most of the period since the Second World War, however, conscription has been a regular feature of public policy. We believe that serious consideration should be given to the feasibility of providing for the regular military defense needs of the country through a voluntary defense force. We favor the use of additional incentives to attract the needed numbers of volunteers. At the same time, we support provisions for conscription as authorized by Congress in time of declared national emergencies. If the president and the Congress should determine that conscription is necessary that decision should be subjected to periodic public scrutiny as to its continued necessity.

We believe that the recent amendment of the Selective Service Act which permits the selection of draftees by an impartial system of random choice and makes possible the limitation of maximum vulnerability to the draft to those between the ages of 19 and 20 is a significant improvement. If conscription must be retained, the Selective Service Act should be amended further in at least the following ways in order to provide increased protection to the registrants:

a. Draftees, determined by an impartial random selection, should be called on a national basis rather than on the basis of a quota established for each local board.

b. Ministerial student exemptions should be repealed. Student deferments should be designed so as to make students, upon completion of a school year, eligible for impartial random selection along with other registrants. Deferments should be continued for specified hardship cases.

c. Occupational deferments should be discontinued except for persons with specialized skills essential for national defense. The granting of such deferments should be carefully scrutinized.

d. Local boards, if they are retained, and appeal boards should include a representative cross-section of the various economic and ethnic concerns and age groups of the area.

e. The administration of the Selective Service System should be revised so as to provide a greater degree of national uniformity in procedures, regulations, and guidelines for the classification of registrants.

f. The procedural rights of individuals should be given increased protection by requiring that each registrant be given a statement of his rights and responsibilities and of the procedures of the Selective Service System; by allowing legal counsel at all hearings and appeals and adhering to normal judicial standards of due process; by providing for legal service to registrants, similar to that of the public defender system; and by permitting prompt judicial review of a contested classification before the person is required to report for induction.

The Congress has provided for alternate service in the case of citizens who object on religious grounds to participation in any and all wars. This provision both affirms validity of religious training that forms the conscience and recognizes that a democracy must protect the personal integrity of its citizens. Such religious training and protection of personal integrity are necessary for the welfare of a democracy. These provisions in the law are a response to the appeals of many religious groups through the years, and now receive the general support of sensitive Americans. We believe it is time now to amend the Selective Service Act so as to provide alternate forms of national service to those who object to war on moral and philosophical grounds other than specifically religious considerations. In addition we believe it is time also to amend the act to provide alternate forms of national service to those who object on religious, moral, and philosophical grounds to participation in a specific war.*

Few judgments of conscience can be made categorically, applying in all times and in all places. Most such judgments are made in reference to particular situations, in light of dominant moral values. The exercise of moral judgment accepts the legitimacy of service in the armed forces. The exercise of moral judgment also requires acceptance of the principle of selective conscientious objection. Furthermore, Christian faith and the Lutheran heritage hold that every person has the right and the responsibility to make his decisions in the love of God, in obedience to his living Word, and in service to his neighbor, not excepting decisions relating to military service. *War, Peace, and Freedom,* adopted by the 1966 General Convention, affirms that a Christian's expected obedience to government policy must not violate his conscience (para. 14). The Christian is personally accountable to God for his moral judgments and actions on matters of public policy.

Alternate service allows a democratic society to respect the claims of conscience without forcing objectors into imprisonment, exile, or a seriously compromised integrity. At the same time the public interest is protected. Claims of selective conscientious objectors should be examined as to their sincerity and depth of moral conviction according to nationally established criteria and uniform procedures.

The ALC encourages Christians to active participation in service to the nation. It teaches the responsibility of all citizens to contribute

---

* Recent regulations announced by the Selective Service Director may already grant alternate forms of national service for those who object to war on social and philosophical grounds other than the specifically religious, but require that the registrant appear before his draft board to convince the board of the sincerity of his views. He also has the right of appeal to his appeals board, and thereafter to the courts.

to the needs of the country in ways appropriate to their skills. The ALC is grateful to its chaplains who minister to those of its members who serve the military needs of the nation. The church also renders pastoral care and understanding to persons in agony of conscience, and pleads that avenues of alternate service be opened to them. Along with the 1968 General Convention, the ALC today "urges its members, and especially its pastors, to counsel with and stand by those who conscientiously object to military service as consistently as they counsel with and stand by those who for equal reasons of conscience serve in the armed forces. It warns against attempts to judge a person's patriotism or his Christian faith by his willingness or unwillingness to render military service" (*Reports and Actions*, p. 486).

D. SERVICE IN THE MILITARY

Compulsory Attendance at Worship Services at Military Academies

The 1964 Convention received a proposed resolution on this issue from the National Lutheran Council requesting the several military departments "to grant complete freedom of choice in matters of religious worship to cadets and midshipmen at their respective academies." After extended discussion and numerous amendments the 1964 Convention adopted the following substitute resolution:

WHEREAS, The American Lutheran Church supports the concern of the United States government for providing worship services at the academies; and

WHEREAS, It has been brought to our attention that cadets at the United States Military Academy, West Point, New York, midshipmen at the United States Naval Academy, Annapolis, Maryland, and cadets at the United States Air Force Academy, Colorado Springs, Colorado, are required to attend religious services; and

WHEREAS, The faith and life of the Evangelical Lutheran Church is distinctive, and its requirements and desires are not met by a general Protestant service; and

WHEREAS, Lutheran worship services are available in the West Point, Annapolis, and Colorado Springs communities, and their continuance is assured for the Lutheran personnel who may choose to attend them; therefore be it

Resolved, That The American Lutheran Church Second General Convention recommend that the National Lutheran Council request the Departments of Army, Navy, and Air Force to grant cadets and midshipmen at their respective academies the freedom to attend available services of their choice in lieu of compulsory attendance of academy chapel services and that the National Lutheran Council through the participating bodies invite the Lutheran Church—Missouri Synod to join with it in this request.

Contact With and for Military Personnel

The 1962 Convention adopted the following five resolutions:

a. Pre-Induction Camp

Resolved, That congregations be encouraged to train and prepare their young people, who inevitably will enter military life, to become witnessing Christians, and that as far as it is practicable the facilities of the 1963 pre-induction camp at Holden Village be used.

b. Communication with Personnel

Resolved, That congregations be urged to keep in constant communication with their members in service and that wherever practicable a referral secretary be appointed.

c. Pastors in Reserve Units

Resolved, That congregations be urged to grant qualified pastors who so desire the opportunity to belong to a local reserve unit and thus reduce to a minimum the number needed on active duty.

d. Service Upon Release

Resolved, That service people and chaplains upon release from active duty be given every opportunity for useful service in civilian communities.

e. Intercessory Prayers

Resolved, That continual intercessory prayers be offered by the church for the people in service and for a durable peace.

Statement by Chaplain Sandrock

By resolution presented from the floor, the 1968 Convention adopted the following: Resolved, That the report of Colonel Hans E. Sandrock during the report of the Committee on Service to Military Personnel be commended to the members of The American Lutheran Church to stimulate their thinking and promote a desire for informed discussion.

Mr. President, Delegates, and Friends of the church. In behalf of all ALC chaplains and servicemen, I should like to express our gratitude and deep appreciation to the church, our esteemed president, Dr. Schiotz, our Chaplains' Chaplain Orlando Ingvoldstad, for your prayers, support, concern, and leadership manifested so amply by Lutheran Service Centers, annual convocations, pastoral staff visitations, the Contact Pastor Program, the Literature Program and for the representation at this convention. You have not neglected us—and we are grateful.

This report will reflect that currently I wear two hats. First, as executive director of the Armed Forces Chaplains Board. Second, as a senior Air Force Chaplain.

As executive director of the Armed Forces Chaplains Board, I serve in the Department of Defense and am on the staff of the Assistant Secretary of Defense for Manpower and Reserve Affairs. Membership in the Armed Forces Chaplains Board is comprised of the three Chiefs of Chaplains, Army, Navy, and Air Force. My duties are to provide direction for the activities of the board and provide liaison between the three military departments. We also maintain liaison between the military departments. We also maintain liaison between the military departments and the Department of Defense. A continuous liaison is also maintained with the Congress, the churches of America and the chaplain endorsing agencies of the churches.

In addition, we generate and coordinate common policies, practices, and programs among the services. As an example, we are responsible for the Religious Education Program for the Armed Forces. This program is called the Unified Religious Education Curriculum. Civilian religious education consultants from the churches of America annually select the best materials published by the Protestant Church-Owned Publishers' Association; Augsburg Publishing House is a member of this Association. These materials are published as received from the churches and distributed throughout the Armed Forces.

At this point I would like to pay a special tribute to four persons from The American Lutheran Church who have represented the church and made outstanding contributions to our servicemen and their dependents. Dr. Richard Evenson has been a consultant on the Unified Curriculum Selection Committee for some years. He is one of our most valued consultants and has represented the church in a most effective manner. Dr. Alida Storaasli has served as a consultant to the Protestant Women of the Chapel. Her excellent leadership and keen insight have been invaluable in the annual preparation of the Women's Resources Guide. Mr. Al Doerring has served in the same capacity as Dr. Storaasli for the Protestant Men of the

Chapel. He will be replaced by Mr. Herb Kent. We deeply appreciate the influence of these great Lutheran leaders and the contributions they have made in our behalf.

Now I wish to speak as an Air Force Chaplain and share a few insights into one of the most exciting, demanding, and rewarding ministries I know—the chaplaincy. In addition to a well balanced pastoral program of preaching, teaching, visits, and counseling, the Air Force accentuates an annual program emphasis. Two years ago we emphasized "The Single Airman Ministry." This program was designed to provide a special ministry to reach the young adult in our military community. Last year the emphasis was "Total Religious Education." This year we are concerned with "The Family." Each of these programs has been enacted in the milieu of the most successful experiment in integration of the races to be found in any segment of our society.

Although laymen are our major concern, we also have unique programs for continuing education for the chaplains. The Air Force provides chaplains with an annual opportunity to attend retreats, seminars and conventions of their respective denominations. Chaplains may also attend annual professional institutes where leaders and theologians of the civilian churches provide information concerning the latest advances in the religious life and thought of America and the world.

Although time precludes a detailed description of the chaplain's work as he seeks to faithfully represent and interpret the Lutheran Church to the Armed Forces, I would be remiss in my duties and unfaithful to our sacred trust if I did not dare risk stating unequivocally the Chaplain's Credo.

You will note the Army Chaplain wears a cross on his lapel, the Navy Chaplain's cross is on his sleeve, and the Air Force Chaplain wears his cross over the heart. These crosses are the symbols of their witness. Many military personnel wear the French Fourragere. The Fourragere is a military decoration presented to a unit for distinguished service and consists of a braided cord worn about the shoulder seam by all the men of the unit which has been honored.

However, the Fourragere was not always a symbol of honor. Mark M. Boatner in his book "Military Customs and Traditions" offers this explanation to its origin. He traces the citation to a hangman's rope and a nail. It seems that a company of soldiers in the Flemish Army belonging to the Duke of Alva was threatened with mass hanging if they did not do better in the next battle. In response to this threat the company exhibited unusual self-confidence by providing the equipment—a scaffold and the hangman's rope. Naturally the next operation was a resounding success and the rope was retained as a unit citation. What originally was meant to be a mark of shame and disgrace became by the power of awakened pride the symbol of splendid and distinguished service.

This analogy should sound familiar to the Christian. Did not St. Paul acknowledge to the Corinthians that the preaching of the cross was nonsense to those who are involved in this dying world, but to us who are being saved from the death it is nothing less than the power of God? The top priority order issued by our supreme Commander-in-Chief states very succinctly, Go—tell it like it is—and love.

Everyone despises war with its senseless slaughter and its idiotic inaneness. We should pray night and day for the abolition of this macabre method of national assertion. But until the day of peace, what do we do?

Dare the churches of this great land say to the soldiers, sailors, marines, and airmen "You go without our blessing" or "We will have none of this"? Lest we forget, there was a Calvary. So long as the world puts men on crosses—the church must put crosses on men. So long as there is conflict—there must be courage. The church must be where the issues are faced—where the action is. At this crucial juncture of history the action appears to be the nitty-gritty of Vietnam. In Vietnam the chaplain is the church. The soldier is the church, the sailor, the marine, the airman is the church. To accompany these men, God's brave choice, to go with them to their battle stations and their lonely places of watchful waiting and vigilance is the chaplain's great privilege and distinct responsibility.

Your chaplain goes with the men not as a hawk, not as a dove, but under the aegis of the American eagle and in the inspiration of the Holy Paraclete which is the Dove of the Spirit.

We too are soldiers, soldiers of America and soldiers of God. The key words of our vocabulary are not politics, tactics, strategy. Our key words are sharing, serving, sustaining. The chaplain's purpose is not to support a war effort, but to support men and women, your sons and daughters who have left home, comforts, and private dreams in answer to the call of the country they proudly, unashamedly call their own, and to which they will return with honest pride. With shoulders straight and head held high, they will always be privileged to say "I Served!"

Although our task can be described in many ways, it has never been said better than in the words of the Chaplain's Credo, "To Bring God to Men and Men to God." The servicemen of The American Lutheran Church join me in a salute to you and the prayer that Almighty God will continue to bless our great church.

E. MILITARY ACTIONS

Cuban Crisis

Meeting at the same time as the Cuban Crisis, the 1962 Convention recessed to hear the address of President John F. Kennedy to the nation and received the text of the statement released by the officers of the World Council of Churches. It addressed a message to President Kennedy and later disassociated itself from the WCC action. The following resolution was adopted.

Whereas, According to the release of the World Council of Churches, three officers of the World Council of Churches speak out against the action of the government of the United States in the Cuban crisis; be it

Resolved, That The American Lutheran Church, assembled in convention in Milwaukee, Wisconsin, on October 24, 1962, inform the officers of the World Council of Churches, the press, and President Kennedy, that we disagree with the statement of the officers of the World Council of Churches and reaffirm our earlier statement of this convention to President Kennedy which is the following:

"The American Lutheran Church, in convention assembled in Milwaukee, Wisconsin, wishes to assure you of its united support in prayer in this hour of national crisis. May the God of peace sustain your strength, grant you wisdom, and guide our steps in the coming crucial days, that an honorable and peaceful solution to the crisis may be found."

Vietnam Involvement

1966 Convention Action: Resolved, That The American Lutheran Church, in the conviction that Christian Americans share in responsibility for national policy, commends the following statement to its members in order to stimulate their thinking, promote a desire for informed discussion, and encourage fervent intercessory prayer.

Along with other churches and religious communities The American Lutheran Church is uneasy and troubled over the United States involvement in Vietnam. To many of us the nation's necessary reliance on military measures should be combined with increased emphasis on social, economic, and political measures in Vietnam.

We know in a limited way of the death, destruction, and misery inflicted upon the people of Vietnam. We know of the sadness that the war has brought to many American families. We know of the cruelty of modern weaponry. We know the dangers of escalation and of a full-scale land war in Asia.

Yet, we know too little of the cruelties and oppression inflicted by the enemies of freedom. We know too little of the true feelings of the people in Vietnam. We know too little of the constructive role the military forces are playing in community building and development of basic public facilities. We have too little information on the subversion and undermining of governments responsive to the people in that land.

We believe that the stated aims of our nation's government in assisting Vietnam are sound. We believe that these stated aims reflect accurately the honest desire of the American people for the welfare of their neighbors in Vietnam. We know that America renounces any claims to colonialism. With other Americans we respect the rights of independent, self-governing nations responsive to the interests of their own people, fully acknowledging their right to establish their own domestic and international policies.

Many of us have an uneasy feeling that our nation's actions may at times belie our stated aims. We do not want our nation to adopt the tactics of deceit, denial of the truth, trickery, and subversion we find so detestable in some other nations. We want our international neighbors to know that the words we speak and the goals we espouse are genuinely the sentiments of the American people, sentiments which guide our international policies, no matter which political party bears responsibility for their administration.

The close of the colonial era, an end which U.S. policies encouraged, has brought the emergence of numerous young nations struggling to establish their independence on strong, economic, social, and political foundations. It appears to us that the communistic governments of Russia and China prefer captive or satellite nations dependent on them rather than genuinely independent nations free to choose courses responsive to their own people.

As one of the world's powerful nations the United States has a heavy responsibility to fill in the world of international politics. We look forward to the day when no one nation alone will have to bear so heavy a burden of international responsibility. We commend those governmental policies which foster and lead to international cooperation for keeping world peace and order.

It would be tragic if our nation were to stifle dissent, muffle criticism of its policies, or refuse to recognize merit and sincerity in the policies of other nations. It is the duty of citizens to express their views to their governmental representatives, criticizing when they feel criticism is due, but also commending, supporting, and sympathizing when such is merited.

As a representative assembly of The American Lutheran Church, we have no special wisdom that enables us to propose specific courses for ending the war. We know and appreciate that our nation's leaders have listened to the voices of the World Council of Churches, the National Council of Churches, the Roman Catholic Church through Pope Paul, and various other organizational voices, and have evaluated carefully the soundness of their counsel. We know and appreciate that our leaders are sensitive to world public opinion, including that expressed in the United Nations. We know and appreciate that our government is seeking to negotiate solutions to our Vietnam involvement.

As an assembly of The American Lutheran Church, therefore, we urge our people to study the issues and express themselves to their leaders in government. We urge our pastors, congregations, individual members, indeed, the nation as a whole, to turn to God in fervent intercessory prayer and genuine repentance for the widespread spiritual apathy presently characterizing our nation, recognizing that even though blame for this conflict is widely shared, nevertheless, no nation involved in its solution has a right to expect to find a sound course of action leading to an end to this or any such conflict apart from such prayer, repentance and spiritual renewal. Let no corporate worship service be complete without the intercessory paragraphs of "The Prayer of the Church," or some adaptations of these petitions for governmental leaders and for world peace. We urge that on Thanksgiving Day and on Christmas Day special additional intercessions be made that God make plain to the leaders of the nations the means by which they might become his agents in bringing to Vietnam and other troubled nations that concord and harmony which we believe God wills for this world.

Vietnam 1968

1968 Convention action: "To approve the statement on "Vietnam 1968" as amended, as a statement of the Commission on Research and Social Action for commendation to the congregations."

The Third General Convention of The American Lutheran Church in 1966 noted its "uneasy and troubled" mind over United States' involvement in Vietnam. Since then there has been a rising toll of casualties, both military and civilian, and a continued diversion of resources from the crises in this country. Further escalation or a prolonged stalemate threatens to increase chances of a major war directly involving the great powers.

The Vietnamese have been struggling for centuries to develop a national identity and to establish their independence. They fought against the French colonial interests after World War II. Their effort is now entangled in the encounter between the conflicting international interests and ideologies of the United States, the People's Republic of China, the Soviet Union and North Vietnam which threatens to destroy the Vietnamese population and culture. The great powers, along with Saigon and Hanoi Governments and the National Liberation Front, all bear heavy responsibility for the present burdens of the Vietnamese people.

An increasing number of Americans are becoming critical of what they regard as a continuing Americanization of the war and its escalation, the high rate of civilian casualties, the limited support given to the Saigon Government by the South Vietnamese people, and widespread corruption among South Vietnamese military and public officials. There is growing anxiety over our country's loss of prestige and moral leadership due to the war. There also are continuing questions of our nation's obligations to treaty provisions which appear to conflict with one another. While many persons support the efforts of the American Government to secure a non-communist South as essential to United States' national interest, others question whether our national interest requires such extensive involvement in the area. Numerous voices are raising serious questions relating to the morality and justice of the conflict.

As delegates to the Fourth General Convention of The American Lutheran Church, we share the above concerns. We do so as loyal citizens, but also as Christians whose first allegiance is to God under whose judgment the policies and actions of all nations must pass. We recognize that military power is necessary for national security. But we believe that the use of military power must be guided by an emphasis on human rights and values, by a desire to provide the stability through which justice and human community can be pursued. The tragic ambiguity of any military action is that it tends to ruin the created order, to subordinate other values to military necessity, and to destroy a nation's population and social order.

We commend the Government of the United States for its unilateral de-escalation of the war which paved the way for the beginning of preliminary discussions in Paris, and urge that every responsible effort be made to secure a cease-fire agreement at the earliest possible date. We support a settlement of the conflict in a manner that recognizes the essential interests of all parties involved, including adequate guarantees for the safety of those who supported either side.

Shifting public moods of optimism and despair do not advance the cause of peace. We caution the members of The American Lutheran Church and our fellow citizens against undue impatience with the pace of the Paris talks and subsequent peace negotiations. The conflicting interests of the warring parties and the uncertainties surrounding our national elections tend to make the negotiating process move slowly. The search for peace involves harsh choices with often imponderable consequences. Our nation is called upon to exercise both determination to establish a just peace and reasonable patience in pursuit of such a peace.

We encourage continued re-examination of the foreign policy of our Government. Public discussion needs to consider the role of the United States in international affairs and the requirements of our national interest. Christians as well as other citizens must share responsibility for helping to define the objectives of foreign policy and to subject its operation to critical review.

In closing our observations on Vietnam 1968, we reaffirm the closing observation expressed by the Third General Convention in these words:

As an assembly of The American Lutheran Church, therefore, we urge our people to study the issues and express themselves to their leaders in government. We urge our pastors, congregations, individual members, indeed, the nation as a whole, to turn to God in fervent intercessory prayer and genuine repentance for the widespread spiritual apathy presently characterizing our nation, recognizing that even though the blame for this conflict is widely shared, nevertheless, no nation involved in its solution has a right to expect to find a sound course of action leading to an end to this or any such conflict apart from such prayer, repentance, and spiritual renewal. Let no corporate worship service be complete without the intercessory paragraphs of "The Prayer of the Church," or some adaptations of these petitions for governmental leaders and for world peace. We urge that on Thanksgiving Day and on Christmas Day special additional intercessions be made that God make plain to the leaders of the nations the means by which they might become his agents in bringing to Vietnam and other troubled nations that concord and harmony which we believe God wills for this world.

Czechoslovakia

1968 Convention action: to adopt the following resolution presented from the floor:

WHEREAS, The Soviet Union has flagrantly violated the rights of the free nation of Czechoslovakia; and

WHEREAS, We deplore this lack of regard for the principles of freedom and self-determination of nations; be it

Resolved, That The American Lutheran Church express deep regret over this action and profound concern for, and sense of kinship with, the people of Czechoslovakia; and be it further

Resolved, That this resolution be communicated to our sister churches in Czechoslovakia: the Silesian Evangelical Church of the Augsburg Confession and the Slovak Evangelical Church of the Augsburg Confession in the CCSR.

V

Race Relations

A. A BASIC STANCE

A Christian Affirmation ...

The Church Council, on recommendation of the Commission on Research and Social Action, in 1961 adopted "A Christian Affirmation on Human Relations." Except for minor textual changes it is identical with a statement adopted by the National Lutheran Council and the three antecedent church bodies in 1958.

WE BELIEVE THAT ...

GOD CREATED one human family and that all men everywhere, whatever their color, culture, class, or caste, are inseparably related and bound together as members of that one human family.

ALL MEN are created in the image of God and are equally precious in his sight.

JESUS CHRIST, himself the God-man, who was born, lived, died, and rose again, lives now as the Savior and Lord of all men everywhere, whatever their color, culture, class or caste.

ALL MEN are by nature selfish and in rebellion against God; and that only through God's reconciling grace can they be set free from the dominion of sin to live as one in Christ.

JESUS CHRIST came to bring salvation to all men; and that, therefore, it is the obligation of the church everywhere to communicate the gospel without discrimination or distinction.

SINCE THE CHURCH is created by God, the decisive factor in its policies and practices is not the will of men as conditioned by social, economic, or cultural patterns but rather the eternal will of God as revealed in Christ Jesus.

THROUGH THE GOSPEL the Holy Spirit establishes the fellowship of believers and to that fellowship calls all men; and that to exclude from worship or membership in the local congregation any person on the basis of color, culture, class, or caste is to sin against God and man.

CHRISTIANS ought to exercise their social responsibility by acting in their own communities to remove whatever injustices exist and to insure for all persons, without discrimination, just and equal opportunities, especially in housing, employment, education, and access to social welfare services.

Effective Ministry in Intercultural Communities*

1964 Convention action: "To adopt the resolution on policy for intercultural ministry reading as follows":

WHEREAS, Inquiries frequently are made as to the policy of The American Lutheran Church respecting various racial and cultural groups; and

WHEREAS, The church's own practices ought to be consistent with its proclamation; therefore be it

Resolved, That The American Lutheran Church adopt the following statement of policy for an effective intercultural ministry as amended, to guide the work of all boards, institutions, auxiliaries, and congregations of The American Lutheran Church.

An Evaluation of Segregation and Stratification

Segregation and social stratification, both based on essentially external differences, regrettably occur in Christian churches. Segregation grows out of many different causes such as tradition, custom, and economics, and is frequently interrelated with man's prejudices, fear, envy, and pride. It is not always easy to discern which is the dominant factor. Segregation often finds its support in differences in skin color or physical appearance. Social stratification is reflected in levels of wealth, education, or social standing. Frequently these man-made distinctions of race and class restrict the ministry of love and belie the fundamental unity of the human race in the redemptive plan of God as revealed in Jesus Christ. The presence of segregation and stratification in the churches hinders the power inhering in the gospel for uniting men through Christ in fellowship with the Father.

In the body of Christ, each person possesses talents peculiarly his

---

* This statement incorporates Church Council actions relative to the enforcement of non-discrimination, the membership clause of congregations, and encouragement to interracial contacts.

own, and each has his unique functions to fulfill, yet all persons are alike in being individually of sacred worth. All are created in the image of God; all stand convicted of sin and in need of redemption; all are invited by Christ to come to him; and God's gift of faith is available to anyone who accepts it. St. Peter was moved, against his own inclinations, to confess, "Truly I perceive that God shows no partiality" (Acts 10:34). St. Paul, describing the Christian fellowship, declared, "Here there cannot be Greek and Jew, circumcised and uncircumcised, barbarian, Scythian, slave, free man, but Christ is all, and in all" (Col. 3:11).

Wherever and whenever the churches help to foster race or class distinctions between people, and wherever and whenever they support attitudes of superiority or inferiority between persons, groups, or classes on the basis of race, class, national or ethnic origin, or economic position they violate God's will. St. James warned against distinctions based on wealth or power, saying, "But if you show partiality, you commit sin, and are convicted by the law as transgressors" (James 2:9).

Congregations, therefore, must avoid segregation and stratification and repent of the evil fruit of natural man's pride and his assumption of superiority over those who are different from him in color, economic position, national origin, or ethnic grouping.

The fact of race and class groupings opens to the church the joy of a ministry that embraces all people without any semblance of exclusion. Under Christ's influence, pride and prejudice are renounced in race and class relations. Snobbery and discrimination are rejected. Jealousy, envy, quarreling, and dissension have no place. The fruits of his Spirit, working in reborn lives, can bring joy, peace, patience, kindness, gentleness, and self-control into the dealings of race with race and class with class.

Were his Spirit to rule in men's hearts and lives, problems of racial segregation and harmful social stratification would diminish. The free and voluntary actions of men who genuinely love neighbor as self because of God's love for them will exceed in justice and equity the compulsory actions forced by decree upon the unwilling.

When persistent and willful rejection of the gracious will of God erodes and destroys a man's willingness and ability to love his neighbor, then the children of God in the orderly processes of a free society must share in the establishment of such justice and equity as are possible in and through the structures of good government in every level of social organization.

It is further incumbent upon Christians, their churches, and their church agencies, so far as it lies within their power, to practice to the full the realistic insights of their faith in dealing with issues of race and class. Assumptions of superiority or privileged position draw the Master's censure today as they did for the sons of Zebedec.

It is the unique task of the churches, shared by every Christian, to seek to bring the power of the word, the sacraments, and the corporate fellowship to bear upon individuals, thereby changing their hearts and lives. The witness of personal and corporate example which treats every person, in every relationship of life, as a human being created in God's image is a powerful testimony to the believer's life in Christ. This course alone promises the ultimate corrective for the evils of segregation and stratification.

Nevertheless, churches, their members, and their leaders need also to exercise Christian social responsibility. They have the duty to protest against and to act responsibly, beginning in their own communities, to correct those cruelties and injustices which deny basic human freedoms. Christians, both personally and corporately, have the duty to press for and to support measures which insure that all persons, regardless of color, economic position, national origin, or ethnic grouping have fair and equal access, for example, to education, housing, employment, voting, and public accommodations.

In times of tension the churches have another duty that makes them especially subject to being misunderstood. They need to stress that with power goes responsibility, that freedoms entail obligations, and that respect has to be maintained as well as attained. Churches cannot become so identified with the cause of any one race or class that they alienate themselves from all others. Their chief purpose is to proclaim the Word. Reform of social structures is a valuable product of such proclamation.

Constitutional Foundation for Action

Consistent with the foregoing viewpoint the Constitution of The American Lutheran Church assigns to the Division of American Missions the objective:

2) To encourage and help existing congregations reach out to all unchurched people in the entire community regardless of race, economic standing, religious background, or other circumstances, in order that they may be brought under the power of the gospel of Jesus Christ and won for him and his Kingdom (p. 42).

Such a mandate is given because this is believed to be in obedience to the word of God, to which The American Lutheran Church submits "as the only infallible authority in all matters of faith and life" (p. 27).

By its Constitution The American Lutheran Church has jurisdiction over its congregations solely for the following purposes:

1) To insure faithful adherence to the doctrines of the Church.

2) To apply discipline when disloyalty to the Church's doctrinal position is evident.

3) To enlist wholehearted cooperation with the program approved by the church (p. 29).

It is to its districts that the church assigns the duty to "exercise general supervision over its clergy, congregations, and conferences" as well as to "consider matters which pertain to the life and program of The American Lutheran Church and present recommendations to the General Convention" (p. 49). The General Convention is empowered to "adopt a program of activity for the church, and take the steps necessary to provide for its accomplishment."

Applications in Specific Policies

Each congregation of The American Lutheran Church is responsible for ministering to the entire neighborhood and area in which it is located. This full ministry of the law and gospel includes the Lord's command to love, to seek out, to evangelize, and to minister to all persons and through the power of the Holy Spirit to bring them into full membership in the church, with all the rights and privileges that inhere in such membership in the body of Christ. Anyone who will respond to the regenerating gospel should be welcomed into the fellowship of the congregation.

All pastors are expected to teach, to support, and to practice the concept of the inclusive ministry. Any pastor who in word and deed denies this Biblical mandate should receive the pastoral counsel of his district president and executive committee.

All boards and departments of the church share in the responsibility for teaching and practicing the concept of the inclusive ministry. Distinctions, preferment, or exclusions based solely on economic, racial, educational, or cultural advantages or disadvantages have no place in the life of the church, or in the establishment of policy.

The occupancy of a particular area for a full-orbed and inclusive gospel ministry, or the relinquishment of such an area ministry, is a question of program and strategy of the entire church. Making the appropriate decision ought not be considered the responsibility solely of a particular congregation or solely of the Division of American Missions. It rather should be a joint decision mutually arrived at after careful consideration of the facts and circumstances affecting each individual situation and the congregations involved.

The district American mission committee is charged to be alert to all mission opportunities in the district and is kept currently informed on the policies, program, and strategy of the Board of American Missions. Therefore, the district American mission committee or departmental committee responsible to the American mission committee shall be expected to counsel with congregations facing the problems and challenges of a changing community. In so doing it may call upon the services of the Board of American Missions, the Division of American Missions of the National Lutheran Council, and such other specialized assistance as may be necessary. Their objective should be to help the congregation to see and to weigh the alternatives before it: whether to leave its present field, whether to accept its opportunities for an inclusive ministry in its present field, or whether simultaneously to occupy and develop a new field while continuing to minister in its present field.

The church exists to win men to Christ and thus to restore the lost into fellowship with the Father. It avoids mere institution-building or the simple perpetuation of a man-made cultural heritage. Should these latter aims supplant the true purpose of the church, or should the opportunities for a significant ministry diminish because of a reduction in the numbers of people reached, the church as a whole has no obligation to provide financial assistance for such a congregation.

Should a congregation willfully and persistently refuse to accept into its membership individuals who in faith and life qualify for membership in a Lutheran congregation, or stubbornly cling to patterns of segregation and discrimination, that congregation should become the object of the pastoral concern of the ALC through the district president and executive committee of the district of which the congregation is a member. The District President also shall report this violation of church practice to the Church Council of The American Lutheran Church. Any pastor who loses his pastorate under such a circumstance should receive the moral and spiritual support of his brethren, and financial assistance from the district for a limited period until he receives a call to a new pastorate.

Clergy from Minority Groups

The 1968 Convention "approved the following substitute resolution."

WHEREAS, The General Convention Committee has received a resolution originating with the National Conference of Inner City Clergy and Laity dealing with "Clergy from Minority Groups"; be it

Resolved, That pastors from the minority ethnic groups in The American Lutheran Church be given equal consideration for calls to congregations and administrative positions of The American Lutheran Church at every level; and be it further

Resolved, That the national president's office work with district presidents in the implementation of this resolution.

Interracial Marriage

1968 Convention action: the following statement on "Interracial Marriage" adopted "as the corporate policy of the church and as a guide to the individual members of the congregations of The American Lutheran Church."

The American Lutheran Church, in "A Christian Affirmation on Human Relations" approved by the Church Council in October 1961 as a policy statement of the church, declared: "We believe that God created one human family and that all men everywhere, whatever their color, culture, class, or caste, are inseparably related and bound together as members of one human family," and that "all men are created in the image of God and are equally precious in his sight."

In 1964 the General Convention reminded members of The American Lutheran Church that "they have the duty to protest against and to act responsibly, beginning in their own communities, to correct those cruelties and injustices which deny basic human freedoms." In 1966 it asked "that we examine ourselves as to what we are thinking, saying, and doing to establish the point that all persons are entitled to equal opportunity in the social order."

We rejoice over the progress toward equality of opportunity in, for example, education, housing, employment, voting, public accommodations, and access to public services. These forward steps can help to bridge the gaps of communication and understanding that so often separate racial and ethnic groups. A major barrier, both real and symbolic, yet remains. That is the barrier to interracial marriage, a social and psychological barrier in many hearts and minds.

We hold that, upon the basis of the gospel of Jesus Christ, a person's race is not a valid ground to deny him marriage to the person with whom he purposes to build a life-long marital union. We confidently affirm that there are no scriptural barriers to marriage across racial lines.

Marriage, however, involves more than the personal decision of two individuals. It is a decision affecting also the parental families, the children of the union, the friends and neighbors, the congregations, and the community. Our convictions on the qualities essential for a wholesome marriage were set forth in "Teachings and Practice on Marriage and Divorce," adopted by the Second General Convention.

Before a man and a woman commit themselves to an interracial marriage they need to examine honestly and openly their own reasons and motivations. They need to examine carefully the probable consequences of their union for themselves, their children, and their families. They need to be convinced that they are sufficiently strong and mature, both spiritually and emotionally, to overcome not only the problems and difficulties normal to any marriage but also the complications added by community attitudes toward interracial marriage. To face these questions adequately they need to enlist the aid of balanced and objective counsel, including that of their pastor.

Should the couple in this light decide that their marriage is one that God can join together, their decision should be honored and respected. Families, friends and neighbors, congregations, and community need to undergird this marriage, as any other, with the sustaining arms of love and fellowship. In particular, the Christian congregation and its members can show how the redemptive, barrier-breaking, gospel releases men from the captivity of ignorance and prejudice. When the interracial marriage is blessed with children the church should take the lead in accepting them, in surrounding them with love and concern, in assisting their parents to "bring them up in the discipline and instruction of the Lord," and in building a climate of public opinion that fosters and guarantees to them every equality of opportunity to develop into mature, self-respecting, respected members of the community.

We neither advocate nor condemn interracial marriage. We rejoice over the diversity in the human family. We understand why persons who appreciate their distinctive racial heritage wish to perpetuate it. Nevertheless, we deny that race must be the determinative criterion in any proposed marriage. Being part of God's creative and sustaining order, marriage builds upon mutual devotion and commitment, mutual recognition and sharing of each other's needs and gifts, mutual strengthening and upbuilding. These qualities know no racial lines.

B. CIVIL RIGHTS AND LEGISLATION

Civil Rights

1966 Convention action: "Resolved, That The American Lutheran Church endorse the following statements as an expression of its conviction and as a stimulus to the thinking and a guide to the actions of its pastors, congregations, and individual members."

The American Lutheran Church believes firmly that equal opportunity for all is a basic civil right which any government must safeguard. To deny equality of opportunity to any person is to deny the revelation of Scripture, the counsel of reason, and the laws of our nation.

The American Lutheran Church therefore reaffirms the convictions it expressed at its 1964 convention, based upon earlier affirmations adopted by it in 1961, and by its predecessor bodies in 1958, principles which are incorporated in its Constitution. "The unique task of the churches," said the 1964 convention, "is to seek to bring the power of the word, the sacraments, and the corporate fellowship to bear upon individuals, thereby changing their hearts and lives." It added a conviction we now reaffirm:

Nevertheless, churches, their members, and their leaders need also to exercise Christian social responsibility. They have the duty to protest against and to act responsibly, beginning in their own communities, to correct those cruelties and injustices which deny basic human freedoms. Christians, both personally and corporately, have the duty to press for and to support measures which insure that all persons, regardless of color, economic position, national origin, or ethnic grouping, have fair and equal access to education, housing, employment, voting, and public accommodations.

Both reason and law support these imperatives. By its Constitution the United States

. . . guarantees that "the citizen of each state shall be entitled to all privileges and immunities of citizens in the several states";

. . . assures all persons within its jurisdiction the freedoms and protections of the first ten amendments known as the Bill of Rights;

. . . confers federal and state citizenship upon all persons born or naturalized in the United States; and

. . . declares that no state has a right to "abridge the privileges or immunities of citizens of the United States," nor shall any state "deprive any person of life, liberty, or property without due process of law, nor deny to any person within its jurisdiction the equal protection of the laws."

The American Lutheran Church rejoices that in the providence of God men were moved to write into the law of the land such powerful protections for human freedom and dignity. Our generation must make these civil liberties a living reality experienced equally by each person within the jurisdiction of the United States.

As a church concerned for the total well-being of every person, we deplore and condemn the racial hostility and antagonism symbolized in the terms "black power" and "white blacklash." Separation, alienation, and rejection along racial lines can become the means by which demonic and alien forces may destroy our nation. We desire a land in which Negro and white, Indian and Oriental, Puerto Rican, Latin American, or person of any other ancestry, may cultivate his abilities, develop his strengths, display his creativity, take pride in his heritage, and win appreciation for his contributions to the common good.

We call upon members of The American Lutheran Church to examine honestly and openly before God our attitudes and actions toward our fellowmen of another race. We ask that we examine ourselves as to what we are thinking, saying, and doing to establish the point that all persons are entitled to equal opportunity in the social order. In so far as we as congregations or individual members may be remiss in this obligation, we should seek the Lord's forgiveness.

Pastors and congregations need to take vigorous, skillful, and patient measures to build bridges of communication and understanding between alienated segments of our society. We need to heed and act upon cries of distress, evidences of exploitation, discouragement of initiative, and denials of opportunities. Rather than limit our involvement to condemning the demonstrations which bring injustices to public attention we need to ask ourselves why we have been so inattentive to and so tolerant of injustices needing correction. Participating with and within the several power structures of our communities, our pastors, congregations, and members need, in their quest for civic righteousness, to work for a social order in which each person has equality of opportunity to develop his potential and to participate constructively in society.

We may differ in our judgments as to which measures or which laws can best guarantee equality of opportunity. Some may argue that conformity cannot be coerced, that it can only be effected by the inner compulsion of the heart. This gives the church two opportunities: (1) through the power of the Holy Spirit to change men's hearts so they will desire to do what is good in the eyes of God, and (2) to win support and respect for laws and ordinances which seek to curb stubborn men as well as others who unthinkingly do what is evil. In these times of domestic stress and strain over civil rights, The American Lutheran Church has no unique wisdom to prescribe the form and content of legislation which may be needed. This remains the task of civil legislators. The church insists, however, that each person is entitled to his birthright of equality of opportunity and equality of protection under the law. No member of The American Lutheran Church, faithful in his commitment to Jesus Christ, can be of an easy conscience before God unless he is actively working to give full effect to this revelation of Scripture, this counsel of reason and these laws of the nation.

Open Housing

1966 Convention action: "To adopt the resolution on open housing as amended."

Resolved, That The American Lutheran Church in convention assembled places itself on record as favoring "open housing," the right of each individual to live where his economic means makes it possible for him to live, without any restriction as to race, creed, color, or national origin.

The achievement of this goal is best accomplished when men of good will voluntarily agree to sell or rent their property to any financially qualified purchaser or tenant.

Where voluntary cooperation is resisted, we believe it lies within the province and responsibility of government—municipal, state, and federal —to adopt such legislation as will discourage prejudicial practices and insure "open housing."

Racism and Political Candidates

1968 Convention action: "to adopt the following resolution":

WHEREAS, The American Lutheran Church has expressed solid opposition to the sin of racism as illustrated by Project Summer Hope (which is the ALC's response in the "crisis" we face as a nation—a crisis of racism so deep that only total effort can hope to remedy the situation); and

WHEREAS, There is grave danger to both the church and society when the church does not speak out positively against the sin of racism, as illustrated by the church in Germany before and during the Hitler era; and

WHEREAS, Many black people and Indians have been and are being lost to Christ and his church partly because the church has acted contrary to her teachings about racism; therefore be it

Resolved, That The American Lutheran Church recommend to its members that they not support those candidates for public office at any level who appeal to racism.

Project Equality

1968 Convention action: "That the statement on 'Project Equality' be adopted as a policy statement."

Project Equality is a program for the religious communions of America developed and serviced by the National Catholic Conference for Interracial Justice. It seeks to use the hiring and purchasing power of religious institutions in an affirmative way to end employment discrimination by making equal employment opportunity a product specification. Thus prospective purchasers in organized religion are expected to evaluate bids from would-be suppliers not only on the basis of price, quality, and service but also on the equal opportunity employment policy and practices of the suppliers.

Besides its praiseworthy declared aims and purposes Project Equality has other positive qualities.

It is interreligious in membership, inviting the participation of churches, synagogues, and related institutions and agencies.
It seeks to provide information, tools, techniques, and procedures by which religious organizations can use their moral suasion and economic power to achieve equal employment opportunity for all persons.
It supplements and reenforces the powers of sound civil legislation.
It recognizes the necessity for affirmative action toward fair employment based on use of skilled expertise, as a means of counteracting unconscious or unintentional discrimination in hiring and promotion practices.
It highlights the purchasing power of organized religion and the economic impact which responsible use of this financial power can exert.
It affirms the obligation of church and synagogue to act in accord with their own teachings on justice and charity to all mankind.

Project Equality commits its participating churches and all of their agencies and institutions to practice equal employment opportunity in their own hiring practices. This commitment requires that the church avoid making religious affiliation a job requirement except for those positions where a religious qualification clearly is a bona fide essential for effective performance of the required duties.

At the same time Project Equality commits its participating religious constituency to concern itself with the employment practices of those manufacturers, distributors, retail firms, and service agencies from whom it purchases materials, supplies, or service. This decision involves commitment, communication of the decision to suppliers, request for a depth response from would-be suppliers evidencing their commitment to the goals of Project Equality, analysis of the responses, and placing of the church's business, with maximum publicity, with firms determined, through Merit Employment Analysis Reviews, to be equal opportunity employers.

Later Project Equality will move as Stage II into the construction industry and the awards of contracts for construction of religious facilities, offering a program to effect compliance and control. In a third stage Project Equality will develop a program to combat racial segregation and discrimination in the employment policies and in the lending and sales practices of insurance, banking, and real estate. Stage III also will concern itself with use of investment portfolios of churches and synagogues in achieving interreligious, interracial goals.

Supervision and direction of Project Equality operations in states or metropolitan areas is effected through a nonprofit interreligious corporation established for this purpose or through a new department of an existing interreligious structure. The national office provides services of research into local discriminatory employment practices, assistance in installing Project Equality in the area and religious constituency, follow-up and consultation services in use of the materials and processes recommended for implementation of the project, coordination of efforts among the various state and local units, provision of factual information on employment practices of specific national industries and firms, and liaison relationships between the religious community and the federal government. It expects to provide to all participating religious institutions the names of firms committing themselves affirmatively to Project Equality, this list expected to be useful in determining future purchasing decisions.

There come times in the history of a nation when certain issues come so compellingly to the fore that they demand forthright action, including the corporate action of organized religion. Currently such an issue is discrimination against persons based on their race or national origin.

Project Equality is one specific proposal and approach for dealing with this currently compelling issue. It encourages, supports, and reinforces respect for law, regard for legal processes, and reliance upon objective information responsibly provided.

The Commission on Research and Social Action recommends that wherever circumstances warrant and the policies and procedures of local units of Project Equality are faithful to the spirit and objectives of the national organization, congregations, districts, and institutions of The American Lutheran Church be encouraged to participate in Project Equality.

Correcting Educational Inequities

A resolution adopted by the Church Council, June 1970, and reported to the General Convention.

WHEREAS, In contemporary life education is one of the most highly significant means for providing access to self-realization, personal dignity and creative involvement in the modern community; and

WHEREAS, Education in inner city schools typically suffers from obsolescent physical structures, inadequate budgets, and deficiencies in adequately trained staff for the particular challenges of inner city communities; and

WHEREAS, Some suburban and rural school districts suffer similar educational deficiencies; and

WHEREAS, Present public support of education in such blighted areas, both urban and rural, is grossly inadequate; and

WHEREAS, The grievous inequities of opportunity which these educational deficiencies generate constitute a serious social injustice; therefore be it

Resolved, That The American Lutheran Church declare its conviction that equality of public educational opportunity shall be afforded all American youth, regardless of geographic or socioeconomic position; and be it further

Resolved, That The American Lutheran Church encourage all its member congregations to vigorously direct their influence toward the redressing of existing injustices by supporting national, state and school district programs designed to end these educational inequities, and by devising volunteer congregational and community efforts to enrich and improve educationally deficient schools.

C. PRICKING THE ALC CONSCIENCE

Minority and Poverty Issues

At a special meeting in February 1968 the Church Council "adopted the following resolutions which resulted in the program called Project Summer Hope and which continues to challenge the concern of The American Lutheran Church":

Resolved, That the Church Council of The American Lutheran Church, speaking for itself, acknowledge the shortcomings of our church in the area of social concern and our insensitivity to the minority and poverty problems of our nation and request the president of The American Lutheran Church to invite suggestions for programs that might be constructively undertaken by The American Lutheran Church and her congregations.

Resolved, That the Church Council request the Board of American Missions, the Board of Social Service, and the Commission on Research and Social Action, together with their respective district committees, and the Board of Trustees to provide such possible assistance and service as may help to meet the needs of those persons who reside in ghettos and poverty stricken areas; and be it further

Resolved, That the Church Council urge the Board of Trustees to authorize an assistant to the president to serve as a liaison person for a period of one year for this particular need.

At its June 1969 meeting the Church Council adopted another statement on "Minority Issues," "recognizing the continuing need for action in our relations with minority groups," and further recommended:

1. That the ALC encourage all its divisions, commissions, departments, auxiliaries, and congregations to continue to give priority to projects initiated under Project Summer Hope and the Omaha convention-authorized national crises fund program.

2. That we challenge the members of the ALC to assume political and economic leadership in developing programs and policies aimed at eliminating injustice and poverty in American society.

3. That the ALC continue and expand the opportunities for conversation between Black, Indian, Hispano, and other minority group leadership and the leadership of the ALC at all levels of our organization.

4. That the Boards of Theological Education, College Education,

and other divisions do all possible to expand opportunities for developing leadership, both clergy and lay, from minority groups.

5. That congregations set up programs of social action, such as tutoring, big brother, big sister, day care centers, housing, and others, particularly endeavoring to involve the youth of our congregations in such projects.

6. That we ask the Commission on Research and Social Action to prepare a study aimed at helping the members of the ALC understand why "law and order" does not always mean the same to all segments of society.

7. That American Missions establish a sponsorship program for Inner City and Rural Crisis programs comparable to sponsorship efforts for World Missions and Church Extension.

8. That the ALC Tenth Anniversary Thankoffering be designated for the ALC National Crises Fund and that Black and other minority people hold significant representation in the group determining the expenditures of this fund.

The Black Manifesto

At its June 1969 meeting the Church Council adopted the following statement relative to "the Black Manifesto."

WHEREAS, The Church Council of the ALC at its annual meeting in June 1969, also considered the "Black Manifesto" and the crisis situation which brought it forth; and

WHEREAS, The Conference for Inner City Ministries meeting in Minneapolis also submitted several resolutions to the Church Council dealing with race relations in which they stated "we oppose any form of violence, any form of destruction, actions that destroy the mind and soul, body and spirit of man": and

WHEREAS, Though we are aware that portions of the "Black Manifesto" are inflammatory, filled with hate, and must be repudiated; that portions advocate overthrow of our government by violence and must therefore be condemned as seditious, we must face the fact that these proposals have arisen because of the anguish and frustration in a segment of our society which feels the hopelessness of oppression and man's inhumanity to man; and

WHEREAS, There exists a need for an informed, sensitive, courageous, and meaningful response by the lay and clergy leadership of the ALC;

The ALC Church Council declares:

A. We are committed to helping solve the American problems of racism and poverty.

B. We know there is no easy way to get the job done.

C. We intend to do those things that we think will help and that we are able to do.

Therefore, the ALC Church Council recommends:

1. That each pastor and church council read the Manifesto carefully in the light of the need to be informed.

2. That each congregation also study the documents that focus on the critical problems of minority groups, race, and poverty and become sensitive and responsive to the needs of minority groups where they live and work.

Unity in Christ

1968 Convention action: to adopt the following resolution:

WHEREAS, The Fourth Biennial Convention has considered many issues on which there cannot be unanimous agreement; and

WHEREAS, These issues were at times discussed with a great deal of emotional fervor; and

WHEREAS, We believe that the body of Christ must not be divided because Christ is not divided, and because he has made us all one, having broken down the dividing walls of hostility; therefore be it

Resolved, That we, the delegates to this convention, pledge our unity in Christ, confessing our love for one another, celebrating our differences of opinion, working together in the furtherance of brotherhood, and following our Lord and Savior in the path of discipleship in service to all mankind.

Priority of Reconciliation

The following resolution, submitted by the General Convention Committee, was adopted by the 1970 convention.

WHEREAS, The president has called attention to the blessings that come from openness to the guidance of the Holy Spirit; and

WHEREAS, The program for the 1970 General Convention provided speakers who focused on the various issues of the day concerning which polarization is evident; and

WHEREAS, There is need for constant renewal in the lives of our membership as well as a continuing sense of responsibility to minister to the healing power of God's grace in the world; and

WHEREAS, The ministry of reconciliation has been given to the church through the revelation of the written Word and Christ, the Word incarnate; therefore be it

Resolved, That The American Lutheran Church, through the corporate congregations and their individual members, attentively and responsibly listen to the voices of those in our society who are alienated, deprived, and otherwise discriminated against; and be it further

Resolved, That the congregations and individual members seek as a priority of concern to exercise the ministry of reconciliation within the congregation and to their community and its segments.

VI

Marriage and the Family

A. THE CHURCH AND HUMAN SEXUALITY

1966 Convention action: "Resolved, That The American Lutheran Church adopt the following statement on 'Sexual Integrity in Modern Society' as its expression of the views which should guide the teachings and practices of its people." To avoid confusion with a study booklet bearing this same title, the Commission on Research and Social Action, under authority granted it by the Convention, retitled the statement "The Church and Human Sexuality."

Sex mores and morals in our day are under the strain of great confusion and critical questioning. The church should accept this confusion and questioning as a challenge to speak out Biblically, forthrightly, and positively. As a church we gladly accept our responsibility so to teach and preach and speak out in matters of sex.

Sexuality is God-given and good (Gen. 1:27; Mark 10:6; Eph. 5:21-33). Human sexuality relates to the whole person. It gives color, tone, and content to the whole of man's or woman's personality and all of his relationships. The physical expression through sexual intercourse is but one of the aspects of our sexuality. The unmarried, too, can find joy and fullness in their manhood or womanhood, apart from this expression.

As with all of God's gifts, sexuality can be warped, exploited, and abused by sinful man. Under the liberating and healing power of the gospel, and within the context of marriage and a genuine interpersonal relationship between husband and wife, sexual intercourse can find its wholesome fulfillment, physically and spiritually, as part of the abundant life for which Christ set us free.

Sexual intercourse finds its proper fulfillment only in marriage. It is indissolubly related to marriage, to the fulfillment of a man's or a woman's life in terms of the most intimate union and companionship known on earth, and to the establishment of a home and the rearing of children.

Healthy sexual attitudes stem primarily from the wholesome experiences, the sound nurture, and the emotional satisfaction of good family life. We urge congregations to provide education for parents to equip them better to exemplify in their lives and to nurture in their children a Christian understanding of sex, its meaning, and its proper use. We encourage sound programs of sex education for parents and for children both in our congregations and in the educational institutions of our communities.

Parental and social pressures currently force dating at too early an age. Until youth are mentally, psychologically, and spiritually able to handle their sexual drives they should avoid situations which promote the arousing of erotic sexual strivings. Too early dating, combined with prolonged economic dependency, easily leads to undesirable sexual experimentation, the exploitation of sexual interests, and premature marriages which cannot withstand the rigors of the years.

We commend the responsible use of medically-approved conception control within marriage for the sound purposes of family planning. We recognize and accept the risk that the widespread availability of contraceptive procedures may lead to increased promiscuity. This fact challenges the church to a positive presentation and a clear affirmation of Christian standards of sexual behavior.

There are times and circumstances when interruption of a pregnancy may be necessary for therapeutic reasons. Such an induced abortion should be undertaken only after adequate consultation with professional persons competent to give trustworthy and balanced counsel. We welcome studies and discussion seeking to determine what may constitute therapeutic reasons for an abortion.

Masturbation is a particular problem during teen-age years because of its frequent occurrence, especially among boys. Social and parental attitudes condemning the practice, while overlooking the factors of loneliness, emptiness, insecurity, or curiosity which may provoke it, may cause shame and guilt and may damage the child's mental health. Medical opinion holds that in and of itself occasional masturbation needs to be seen as neither abnormal nor detrimental to health. It becomes disturbing when it is an end in itself, an obsessive practice, or a symptom of warped sexuality.

Pornography tends to create an unhealthy preoccupation with sex as an end in itself without the responsibilities of a continuing relationship. Such a self-seeking, debasing attitude is contrary to that self-giving Christian attitude which sees sexual expression in relation to the whole person and which demands sublimation of the sexual drive except in the marriage relationship. (See 1 Cor. 6:15-20.) We endorse responsible efforts to curb pornography, which endangers persons, disrupts wholesome sexual fulfillment, and corrupts values protecting marriage, the family, and communities.

Medical and psychiatric advice leads us to view homosexuality as an immaturity or an illness which can be treated and sometimes cured. We reaffirm our belief that homosexuality is contrary to God's will for the proper use of sexual drives. Nevertheless, we agree that the homosexual should be regarded as a person in need of help and healing for his warped sexuality. He may find in the redeeming strengths and influence of Christian fellowship, fed by the means of grace, the power for a changed way of life. We do not condemn him, but we do not condone his behavior.

Where a sexual problem or abnormality gives rise to marriage crises and family difficulties we encourage the persons involved to seek pastoral counsel or the help of Lutheran social services or other qualified professional counselors in the community. Persons in such difficulty are encouraged to seek help early rather than to wait until difficulties become critical, so that the healing love of God can come sooner and with greater opportunity for solution. Then those helped should express their gratitude to God and his agents of reconciliation and healing.

In our homes and churches we need to teach with renewed intensity the beauty, the joy, the emotional satisfactions, and the healthy contributions which sexuality adds to human experiences and family living. We need to underscore the protections both to persons and to society which follow when our sexuality is placed under the directing disciplines of obedience to God and respect for neighbor. The world needs to hear our testimony that when—and only when—sexuality is used as directed by God it becomes an expression of his providential goodness and his blessing upon humanity.

B. TEACHINGS AND PRACTICE ON MARRIAGE AND DIVORCE

1964 Convention action: WHEREAS, Pastors and parishioners desire clarity and a greater measure of consistency in teachings and practices concerning marriage and divorce; and

WHEREAS, A clear and convincing voice of the church is needed to witness against abuse of marriage and divorce; and

WHEREAS, The basic viewpoints set forth in a preliminary draft issued by the commission were widely studied within the ALC and overwhelmingly endorsed as soundly evangelical; therefore be it

Resolved, That The American Lutheran Church adopt the following statement on "Teachings and Practice on Marriage and Divorce" as a valid expression of evangelical Christian views; and be it further

Resolved, That all pastors of The American Lutheran Church be encouraged to teach and practice these views insofar as they are consistent with their own Spirit-enlightened consciences, and be it further

Resolved, That the norms reflected in this statement be incorporated into the teaching materials issued by any boards and departments of The American Lutheran Church.

Marriage

The Foundation for Marriage

Marriage is an institution ordained by God with the creation of man. Its structure rests in the creation of man as male and female (Gen. 1:27). Sexual differences are of God's good design, intended to bring joy and enrichment to human life as well as to provide for procreation. The essence of marriage is that in the act and relationships of marriage two persons become one flesh (Gen. 2:24). In this complementary nature of the two sexes as God created them lies the basis for marriage and each new family.

Marriage exists within a world which is characterized by alienation from God and from fellow man, and therefore is affected by the sinfulness of man. Nevertheless, being part of God's creative and sustaining order, marriage as an institution continues to exist under God's goodness and protection. It provides the framework within which children are nurtured and trained for living with their fellow men. Laws, regulations, and customs which order and control marriage are a social and moral necessity, and, when rightly drawn and administered, they fill God's good purposes.

Christian people will recognize their marital union as belonging to God's order of creation. They will seek also the fulfillment of their marital union in Christ as they grow in loving one another even as Christ has loved them, as they learn to forgive one another in the spirit of Jesus Christ, and as they draw upon the resources which the Lord of the church makes available to his people.

The Unity of Marriage

The devotion to one another and the unity named in Gen. 2:24 are of the essence of marriage. Husband and wife become a paired unity—in sexual expression, in values and goals, and normally in parenthood. They ought to become a harmony of personalities, a couple belonging together, "No longer two but one" (Mark 10:8).

This oneness of husband and wife, marked by unwavering lifetime fidelity, is compared in Scripture to the oneness of Christ and his church. The husband is to love his wife as Christ loved the church and gave himself for her. Each yields to the other full devotion and selfless consideration. It is on this exalted level that conjugal rights and obligations are granted and accepted. Neither lords it over the other nor insists selfishly on his rights and the duties owed him. Together husband and wife become one in love. (See Gal. 5:22, 23; Eph. 5:21-25; Col. 3:18, 19; 1 Peter 3:1-7.)

Every person has been created by God with gifts that make him a unique personality. The strength and unity of marriage come from mutual recognition and sharing of each other's needs and gifts. This unity recognizes the freedoms of husband and wife to express their own interests as well as their duty to share in those relationships where sharing is essential to the success of the marriage.

Love in Marriage

As God is love, so has he given to male and female, created in his image, the capacity to express love, even if this capacity may have been damaged in the experiences of life. Marriage can be the prime opportunity through which man can express the divine relationship of love. That love which partakes of divine love is mature, kind, considerate, self-giving, dedicated to the well-being and the fulfillment of the other as of himself, and faithful to the beloved until death. Its characteristics are described in 1 Cor. 13:4-7. It patterns after that perfect love which God manifests in his mighty acts. Its characteristic is to give rather than to get. This love is the way of life in marriage, the quality in which the marriage partners ought to grow and mature.

Sexual intercourse should be an expression of love, but love is both richer and more inclusive than the sex act. Sexual harmony, truly one of the joys of marriage, nevertheless is not so much the goal of marriage as it is a reflection of the total unity and love of the married pair. In an age which falsely portrays and exploits sex and love, many couples become disappointed with sex as they experience it. Major marital problems may stem from or be reflected in such unwholesome experience with sex.

A marriage becomes a distinctively Christian marriage through faith in the creative love of the Father, the redemptive love of Jesus Christ, and the sanctifying power of the Holy Spirit. Even the marriage of Christians, however, daily falls short of the Christian ideal. Hence the Christian husband and wife daily need God's forgiveness for their sins of omission and commission, followed by a readiness to be forgiving toward each other. In gratitude to God they daily rededicate themselves to him and to one another, realizing that their marital unity is never completed but is always in the process of becoming.

Preserving the Marriage

Problems are normal to marriage. They can be turned into stepping stones to mature marital unity or they can become stumbling blocks to wreck the marriage. When people become involved in marital difficulties, it should be a concern of pastors and of relatives and friends to provide help and understanding in overcoming the conflicts, thereby strengthening and preserving the marriage. The total costs of disruption of a marriage are high, not only for the principals but above all for the children. Broken marriages are destructive also of family, congregational, and community strength. Therefore couples having difficulties in their marriage should be helped to find competent counsel in ample time before the marriage itself is threatened.

Marriage, obviously, is more than a legal state entered into through prescribed steps; it also is a continuing process of growth toward marital unity. Even before entering the estate of matrimony, by meeting its legal requirements, a couple has begun the process of building a marriage. The more clearly people comprehend this view of the estate of matrimony the more willingly they may strive to realize its benefits for themselves and for those near and dear to them.

Divorce

The Nature of Divorce

Divorce, too, is both a legal state and process. When two persons find their relationship as husband and wife increasingly intolerable the process of alienation has begun. If the two meet the legal requirements for divorce this alienation could lead to divorce. But, divorce needs to be seen realistically as the breaking of an order of God, the public admission and the legal recognition of an already broken marriage, the culmination of a process of alienation.

Such a broken relationship is an evidence that either or both persons were unable or unwilling to grow and mature in conquering selfishness, in accepting patiently the faults and shortcomings of the other, or in meeting the tensions of modern life. For these or other reasons they were unable to fulfill God's will and plan for marriage.

Divorce, according to the teaching of Jesus, is a concession to the fact and reality of sin in a fallen world. Being the friend of sinners, Jesus did not condemn or drive away a divorced person. Neither did he excuse divorce. Rather, he declared "What therefore God has joined together, let not man put asunder" (Mark 10:9). He spoke no word by which a man or a woman might rationalize his divorce into a righteous act. Jesus did, however, explain divorce as resulting from the hardness of men's hearts (Matt. 19:8; Mark 10:5). Divorce arises from self-centeredness or other obstacles the couple cannot or will not overcome.

Appraising Grounds for Divorce

Divorce unfortunately is a reality, a consequence of human sinfulness. The legal dissolution of a marriage sometimes is the lesser of several evils. Adultery and willful desertion often are regarded as valid grounds on which a Christian may seek or accept a divorce. These two "biblical grounds" (based on Matt. 5:31, 32; Matt. 19:9; 1 Cor. 7:10-15), however, cannot be offered as a mechanical rule or a binding law, for neither exception is given in Mark 10:11, 12 or Luke 16:18. Moreover, continuing cruel, calloused, or gross selfishness, the very opposite of the divine principle of love, can as fully wreck a marriage as do adultery or desertion.

Regardless of the legal decision of guilt, each party generally bears some responsibility for the failure of the marriage. The legal grounds indeed may not even be the actual grounds for divorce. In addition, some marriages may be dissolved by annulment which in other legal jurisdictions would be ended by divorce. These facts illustrate why the church must follow an evangelical rather than a legalistic approach to the problems of divorce.

For two earnestly, genuinely Christian persons to seek divorce is almost unthinkable in light of the teachings of the New Testament. Christian spouses normally elect to endure wrong, suffering, and hardship, praying and working for the restoration and strengthening of their marriage. Certainly before they commit themselves to a divorce they will undergo a trial period of separation from bed and board, thus giving themselves time and opportunity to evaluate the total costs of the possible termination of their marriage, both for themselves and for any children they may have.

Ministering to the Divorced

Members of the church are urged to show love and Christ's spirit of forgiveness toward divorced persons. These persons should not become the victims of gossip, ostracism, or undue attention. They need rather to be brought to feel anew the bonds of human fellowship and the sense of God's continuing presence, so that their divorce, unfortunate as it is, nevertheless may lead toward a more mature Christian life. The means of grace remain freely open to them.

True to her mission, the church is in the world to seek out, to serve, and to save sinners. She owes the sinner the clear proclamation of God's law and his gospel of forgiveness. Faithful servants of Christ will seek to help any person laboring under feelings of guilt, rejection, distress, and anxiety with God's word of healing love. To be forgiven and fully restored to fellowship with God and his people, the person involved in divorce needs truly to forgive his former spouse, to recognize his own sins as such, to repent of them sincerely, and in all humility to ask God's forgiveness and strength for a better life.

Remarriage

The Word of God nowhere gives specific permission for the remarriage of a divorced person. Indeed, Jesus' words regarding the institution of marriage and Paul's words in comparing marriage to the relationship of Christ and the church may lead a Christian to believe that if he has passed through the experience of a divorce he cannot remarry during the lifetime of his divorced partner. On the other hand, divorce is nowhere listed in the Bible as an unforgivable sin. Moreover, a person who has had the traumatic experience of a divorce may need desperately the love and companionship of marriage. The fact of a divorce does not change the verdict of Scripture that "It is not good that the man should be alone," nor the reality of temptation which is acknowledged by Paul in his statement "It is better to marry than to burn." Therefore any Christian who is contemplating remarriage after divorce must give full and prayerful consideration to the entire witness of Scripture before making his personal decision in this matter.

The church is concerned for the total well-being of persons in time as well as in eternity. The pastor deals with the problem of remarriage not in isolation but in the context of the church's total stewardship of the gospel. He takes into account relevant factors involved in the lives of the two individuals, any children they may have, the well-being of congregation and community, the cause of good order in the church, and the responsible freedom with which he and his brother pastors are entrusted.

The remarriage of a person whose previous marriage was terminated by death normally can be commended as a sound decision, renewing the blessings of companionship which a good marriage brings. This is as true for persons in the years of retirement as for those in the years of young adulthood or middle age.

Recommended Pastoral Practice

Positive Programs of Education

In light of current trends and pressures positive Christian education and preparation for marriage and family life belong in every pastor's ministry. He should be alert to opportunities in the pulpit, home, church schools, confirmation classes, and auxiliaries for influencing commitment to Christian standards in the choice of a marriage partner and in patterns for marriage and family living. In counseling sessions he can lead persons to see the implications of their Christian commitment for the marriage and family relationships they are experiencing. He should encourage the members of his congregation to assume a constructive attitude toward the preservation and strengthening of marriage.

Considerations Before Any Marriage

When he officiates at any marriage the pastor acts not only as an agent of the state but also a servant of Christ. Therefore he should satisfy himself that both the man and woman desiring to be married know what is required in marriage and earnestly intend by the help of God to live up to its obligations. Normally he should require that the couple participate in a program of premarital education. If the pastor, in clear conscience before God, is not convinced that this couple is ready to enter upon a responsible marriage he should be supported by his congregation in his refusal to perform the desired marriage.

Particularly difficult is the request to officiate at the marriage of a man and a woman markedly different in such characteristics as religion, race, age, and cultural background. Such a marriage presents complex problems fraught with difficulties. The pastor should insist that the couple examine carefully the consequences of their marriage for themselves, their children, their families, their congregations, and their community. Only when the pastor is firmly convinced that the two are sufficiently strong and mature, both spiritually and emotionally, to overcome the hazards to a sound marriage which their marked differences in background, experience, and outlook impose, should he officiate at the desired marriage.

In situations where young or immature persons, under pressure of an unexpected pregnancy, seek to be married, the pastor may counsel strongly against marriage, which is an estate for adults able to accept its obligations. He may point out that to marry may be to compound an already difficult situation. Adults ought not to insist that the youth be married, whether "to give the baby a name" or for other face-saving reasons. When marriage of the couple is not desirable the pastor should work in consultation with an appropriate social agency to see that the needs of the couple are adequately met and the interests of the child are protected.

Remarriage of a Divorced Person

Should a divorced person approach a pastor for his services in a new marriage, The American Lutheran Church counsels caution. The pastor should avoid taking either a lax or a legalistic stand on possible remarriage, rather being guided by the highest evangelical considerations. He should see the issue in relation to the gospel, life in the Christian community, the polity of his church, and his relations with his brother pastors. He should ascertain through careful pastoral inquiry whether reconciliation with the former spouse is possible, whether this person has come to an understanding and repentance for what he may have contributed to the failure of his former marriage, whether he now has a genuine understanding of what the estate of matrimony requires, and if he has the spiritual maturity to accept its obligations. Unless he believes that the grace of God can become truly operative in this marriage, for the healing of hurts and the strengthening of weakness, the pastor should not lend his office to the desired marriage.

Citizenship Responsibility

Each pastor should inform himself on the marriage and divorce laws of the state or province in which he ministers. He also should take an informed interest in any family life education programs which may be conducted in the public schools as well as in the work of agencies supporting family life in the community. All pastors, as well as their members, should support sound legislation both to foster high standards for marriage and the family and to correct the evils and abuses which much divorce legislation now condones.

Summation of Our Position

The church dare never be lax in her teachings on marriage as a holy estate, to be held in honor by all. She dare never give the impression that she excuses or condones divorce or rationalizes divorce into a righteous act. Nevertheless, the church strives to understand divorce and the problems of divorced people. She attacks the problem of divorce not through negative criticism or repressive legislation but by the persistent and faithful teaching of positive Christian principles of marriage and family living. In her ministry to the divorced person she strives to be not punitively legalistic, but understandingly evangelical, as was her Lord to the Samaritan woman at the well (John 4:16-18). The genuine remedy for the ills of divorce lies ultimately in the better control, guidance, and support of marriage toward the plans and purposes the Creator himself designed and which his people want to uphold and to magnify.

C. THE ABORTION QUESTION

Therapeutic Abortion

The Executive Committee of the Church Council in 1963 submitted the following statement on "Therapeutic Abortion" "as a help to the members of The American Lutheran Church."

The Commission on Research and Social Action of The American Lutheran Church has prepared a preliminary statement on therapeutic abortion for the study and critical comment of nineteen district committees on research and social action. This is preparatory to a possible position paper for the guidance of church members.

Meanwhile, some state legislatures are presently considering revision of the laws governing abortion. Pending the completion of the studies of the Commission on Research and Social Action, the Executive Committee of the Church Council submits the following statement (incorporating a part of the preliminary statement of the Commission on Research and Social Action) as a help to the members of The American Lutheran Church.

1. Therapeutic abortion presents complex problems involving such areas as ethics, morals, psychology, psychiatry, economics, sociology, the law, and theology.

2. Responsible consideration has generally been given to the medical, surgical, and legal aspects of the problem of abortion. Provision is made in all accredited hospitals for medical and surgical consultation in such surgery. Most states have laws governing legal procedures in abortion. Seldom, however, is adequate provision made for the systematic consideration of the other facts of the complex problem of abortion.

3. Therefore, it is the opinion of the Executive Committee of the Church Council that persons facing the question of abortion should be confronted with the many ramifications of the operation and be given effective assistance in working through the problems involved.

4. When therapeutic abortion is contemplated, the factors involved other than the medical and surgical operation pose problems which must be faced earnestly. Consideration of these problems may disclose risk-taking greater than that which is to be avoided by the abortion.

5. A decision whether or not therapeutic abortion should be done should be by a consensus of a committee consisting of a hospital staff surgeon, obstetrician, internist, psychiatrist, and authorized representative of the faith confessed by the patient.

6. In our judgment therapeutic abortion is permissive when:

    a. the life of the mother is involved;

    b. where the mother's health is threatened with severe physical or mental impairment;

    c. but not in cases of possible deformity (a few years ago popular opinion condemned Hitler for proposing euthanasia for deformed people).

In no instance is personal convenience a proper consideration. Always both patient and doctor are faced with the question: Is not termination of pregnancy in this way a transgression of the Commandment "Thou shalt not kill"?

Man lives by his accountability to God. God, who has given life, reserves for himself the right to take life. Any person who asks for a therapeutic abortion or who participates in the decision to carry it out must be sure that he does it in the name of God, certainly in accountability to God.

Abortion, Christian Counsel, and the Law

Based on reactions to a number of preliminary drafts of proposed position statements, beginning in 1962, the Commission on Research and Social Action and the Church Council submitted to the 1970

General Convention a statement on "Abortion, Christian Counsel, and the Law." The Convention, after reaffirming its 1966 stance on abortion, requested the Commission, in consultation with the Theological Council, "to develop and circulate for study and discussion a new statement respecting abortion which places it in a larger context, provides clearer guidance for pastoral counselling, and takes into account the observations expressed in convention discussions on 'Abortion, Christian Counsel, and the Law.'"

D. WHEN DEATH COMES

The Church Council in 1965 approved for release a statement prepared by the Commission on Research and Social Action and the Commission on Worship and Church Music relating to a realistic facing of death, funeral practices, and comfort to the bereaved, under the title "Appointed Once to Die."

Life and Death

Life and death are inseparable. The values a person holds in life will affect his attitudes toward death. What he is willing to die for tells much about what a person thinks it important to live for. Though death may come at any moment, man dare not let the fear of death paralyze his life.

Formed in the womb, and sooner or later laid away in the tomb, man will rise again, either to serve with the saints or to despair with the damned. Birth and death are but personal milestones on the paths of eternity. Life is from God. Death is the prelude to the resurrection.

During his days on earth the Christian lives and moves and has his being in Christ. He commits himself to his Lord's cause. He purposes to express his saving faith in a ministry of service to persons (Eph. 2:8-10). He knows that whether he lives or dies, he is the Lord's. The end of his earthly existence gives to the Christian the crown of victory.

Men who do not know Christ may find life as empty as Job 3 and Ecclesiastes 3 describe it. Psalms 37, 90, and 130 sing of victory over injustice and oppression in this life. The Christian's trust that death is conquered comes from God's Word in such chapters as John 11, Romans 5, 1 Corinthians 15, 2 Corinthians 4, Hebrews 11, and Revelation 5 and 7.

Ready to Die

So assured, the Christian embraces the joy of life even while prepared to leave this earthly sphere whenever death comes. He keeps himself close to the saving presence of the Good Shepherd, walking in his way to life. He is at peace with God and man, repenting and forgiving, trusting and loving.

His earthly affairs ought always to be in order. He should have his will current, in proper legal form to permit handling of his estate according to his Christian convictions. His financial status should be known to his spouse and next of kin. His insurance, pension, social security, veterans service, citizenship, and other records should be up-to-date, readily at hand in an agreed-upon place, which normally—depending on the laws which govern—would *not* be a bank safe deposit box. The dates of baptism, confirmation, marriage, and other biographical information should be recorded. His wishes for his own funeral ordinarily should be discussed with those who are expected to arrange his burial.

Most Christians are given earth burial, in keeping with ancient customs of the church. To others, a reverent cremation seems consistent with the process of "dust to dust and ashes to ashes." Some who die at sea of necessity are committed to the deep. What matters is the promise that in the resurrection the Lord will raise up all who die in the faith in new imperishable spiritual bodies bearing the image of the man of heaven (1 Cor. 15:42-50).

Perhaps the Christian will wish that at death his eyes or other organs be removed and given to strengthen another person. He may even desire to offer his body for medical research or training. Such proposed acts, intended in charity to fellow man, he should discuss prayerfully with his family, pastor, and doctor. Should he decide to take one or the other of these steps he should fill out the proper forms to authorize such action.

It is wise to anticipate the possibility that the circumstances associated with his death may require or urge an autopsy. If competent medical counsel so requests, the survivors readily should give approval. Thereby they may advance medical knowledge and the care and treatment of the sick and suffering in this world.

Provided that the family is likely to remain in the community rather than to join the ranks of mobile Americans, a careful preneed choice of burial plot may be a wise family decision. Advance discussions with a funeral director about legal requirements to be

met and costs and services involved in funerals should prove enlightening. Contracts and financial commitments for burial services,
however, generally should be avoided until the need arises for these
services.

When a serious illness or accident strikes a parishioner, the pastor
should be notified. As a minister of the healing Savior he can speak
the timeless Christian message to the needs of the moment.

When Death Comes

Notify the pastor immediately when a member of the congregation dies. No matter what the hour, the pastor wants to share the
sorrow of his people and to comfort and strengthen them through
the gospel.

Enlist the experience and counsel of the pastor in making burial
arrangements. He should be the first to aid the family in planning a
Christian funeral. Final plans for the funeral should not be made
until the pastor has been consulted.

Engage a funeral home whose personnel understand the spirit
of a Christian funeral to call for the body, to conduct the arrangements worked out in consultation with the pastor, to complete
needed legal papers, and to publish the obituary notices.

Notify employer or employees, executor of the will, insurance
companies, banks, attorney, governmental offices, social security administration, retirement board or pension group, etc., of the death,
requesting forms for filing claims or closing accounts. The funeral
director, on request, will help in this task.

Plan a funeral which reflects the choices and values, standards of
living, and sense of proprieties of the family. Good taste, Christian
consideration, and respect for the deceased should rule the decisions
made.

Respect the honesty and dignity of death in preparing the body
for burial. There is no need to erase the lines of toil or the marks of
age. What is necessary is to bear witness to the reality of the fact
that the deceased has departed this earthly life.

Arrange opportunity for friends of the deceased to visit the survivors, expressing their sympathy, love, regard, and concern. Prior
to the funeral service the casket may be open, the body lying in
state for mourners to view the earthly remains.

Suggest ways in which those closely associated with the departed can express appreciation for what he meant to them. Flowers
symbolize such beauty of association. Contributions made to church,

charitable, educational, medical, or civic causes dear to the departed also express tangibly the esteem in which he was held.

Request the pastor to conduct a brief, private, devotional service for the family and friends, perhaps during the visitation period on the evening before the funeral, perhaps shortly before the funeral service, or as the specific circumstances suggest.

The Funeral Service

The funeral service for a Christian who dies in the faith normally should be held in the church, under the direction of the congregation and the leadership of its pastor. This is so because:

The Order for the Burial of the Dead, prescribed by the church, is a Christian service speaking the faith, joy, and assurance of the church, rather than a eulogy on the life or a display of the bodily remains of the deceased;

The funeral is a public expression of Christian solidarity when death comes to a member of the Christian community. As an act of congregational worship the funeral service provides opportunity for prayer and praise, readings and responses, hymn singing, a sermon speaking to the living the way of salvation found only in Jesus Christ, and a public confession of victorious, triumphant faith;

The music, placement and closing of the casket, number and arrangement of flowers, and all other elements of the funeral service can be controlled so as to reflect the teachings and practices of the church;

The church edifice with its baptismal font, altar, communion rail, cross or crucifix, lectern, pulpit, and visual symbols, so meaningful to the deceased in life is the proper place for the service from which his earthly remains are laid to rest;

The Christian funeral conducted in the church edifice is a powerful Christian witness to neighborhood and community of God's word of hope and resurrection.

The funeral service should be conducted by the pastor of the congregation of which the deceased was a member. If the service is held in a church not served by this pastor, arrangements to this end should be made with the pastor of that congregation. Any other pastor may participate in the service only after prior consultation with and by agreement of the pastor who is in charge of the service.

The hymns sung by the congregation and all other music in the funeral service should proclaim the resurrection faith of Christian people. Neither songs of mere sentiment nor secular music have a place in the Christian funeral. The pastor's counsel on appropriate hymns and music should be followed.

In making arrangements for the time of service, consideration should be given to a morning hour, even though in many communities an afternoon funeral is more typical. Members of the congregation should be encouraged to attend the funeral of a fellow member, thus demonstrating the reality of the Communion of Saints.

At times, of course, good and compelling reasons require that the service be conducted in the family home or in a funeral home. God's clear and powerful word of comfort and hope can give strength and assurance to the mourners in this setting as truly as when it is spoken in the sanctuary. Even in this setting the Order for the Burial of the Dead should be used for one who dies in the faith. A brief form of the Order, available from Augsburg Publishing House as a leaflet *I am the Resurrection and the Life,* may be distributed so that all who are present can participate in the service.

The casket shall remain closed during the service. The rubric of the *Service Book and Hymnal* (page 253) directs that the casket be placed lengthwise (vertical) to the altar. This reflects the church's tradition that the altar symbolizes the east and that resurrection will come from the east. Unless practical requirements dictate otherwise, this placement of the casket should be the normal procedure. Flowers should be discreetly located so as not to obstruct the view of the altar, pulpit, etc. Where practicable, only the flowers of the immediate family should be placed in the chancel of the church.

The casket may be covered with a funeral pall furnished by the congregation. The pall symbolizes a blanket of blessing bestowed by the church as well as the shutting out of earthly things. For a member of the armed forces the flag may replace the pall.

The committal service is an integral portion of the Order for the Burial of the Dead. In no case shall this Order be interrupted by the symbols, rituals, or exercises of secular organizations. Neither should flags be carried into the church as a part of the funeral procession.

Both during the hours of visitation and in the hours around the funeral service members of the congregation should offer their help to the bereaved in the many seemingly small but exceedingly meaningful things that Christian love finds to do. Perhaps the congregation may arrange to serve refreshments or a meal, either before or after the service. Every such symbol of Christian solidarity gives opportunity to friends and relatives of the deceased to share in the supporting warmth and strength of Christian fellowship.

The Loneliness of Grief

Grief at the passing of a loved one is both natural and normal. Even Jesus wept at the death of Lazarus (John 11:35). Death brings loneliness and emptiness. One with whom so much was shared no longer is sharing with us. Ties and relationships, even for the unmarried, have been broken. Until new ties have been made and alternate relationships established, grief and loneliness will be strong.

Guilt, bitterness, and hostility often overpower the survivors, especially in sudden or accidental death. Mean questions nag them: Could I have caused him to die? Did I do all I could to prevent it? Was he still resenting my cruel remarks or actions? How can I make amends for my misdeeds to him? Why did he desert us now? What kind of a God would let this happen? When such feelings torment the survivors they need the help and counsel of their pastor.

The bereaved also need the help of Christian friends in overcoming grief. Their need continues not just for hours, but for days, weeks, even months. They need understanding persons with whom they can share the burdens of their hearts and minds. They need someone with whom to relive the joys and the sorrows, the hopes and the realities, the doubts and the certainties of the relationship now ended. The support and strength which good Christian friends bring to the grieving can turn their sorrow into a healing, restoring experience.

Thus unburdened the bereaved will be able to build new ties, establish new relationships, and once again take a meaningful place in the life of the congregation and community. For them the intercessory petitions in the Prayer of the Church, "Bring consolation to those in sorrow or mourning," and "We remember with thanksgiving those who have loved and served thee in thy church on earth, who now rest from their labors," as well as the church's confident testimony of All Saints Day take on an ever-new depth.

Every Christian has the duty and the joy so to aid his bereaved brothers and sisters in the Lord to overcome their feelings of grief and guilt with the power of the Holy Spirit. His message of confident trust and total victory through Jesus Christ sustains and comforts the Christian. Those who die in the faith know that they will join all of God's saints in the new heavens and the new earth (2 Peter 3:13).

VII

Social and Economic Life

A. TELEVISION PROGRAMMING

Responding to a 1968 Church Council assignment, the Commission on Research and Social Action and the Commission on Public Communication jointly developed the following statement on "Violence in Television Programming." It was adopted by the 1970 Convention "as a statement expressing the judgment and corporate conviction of The American Lutheran Church as its contribution to the discussions seeking an informed solution to a difficult problem of contemporary life and society."

Regarding Violence

We assume that most members of The American Lutheran Church define "violence" as essentially the "amoral aggressive use of physical force, bringing bodily injury to persons or damage to or destruction of their property." We share their concern over the possible effects which the portrayal of violence may have upon the attitudes and actions of viewers and upon social values.

We believe, further, that the concept of violence should be extended to include (1) psychic injury, (2) any systematic degradation or dehumanization of any persons or classes of persons, as well as (3) any systematic exclusion from or denial of opportunity to persons on account of their race, religion, national origin, or socioeconomic status, and (4) the severely disproportionate depictions of life, which lead to false and misleading conceptions of reality.

Violence is essentially a poor and ineffective, even self-defeating, way of handling conflict between persons and groups. It is a process which actually can become socially destructive. It may lead to insensitivity to the problems and sufferings of others, and to an immunization of people and society against the just claims of others upon them. Rather, we search for and advocate alternate patterns of relationships which build upon love and concern, such alternate patterns serving to redirect man's aggressive drives and rechannel his frustrations.

Yet, we recognize that at least the threat to use force may be necessary for a just social order—and that the threat to use must be credible, must even be exercised to be fully credible. But, force thus used as a last resort, either as a means of maintaining order or of securing and preserving cherished values, appears to sanction the use of violence and stimulates violent reaction. Any realistic approach to violence on television must take into account a balanced, whole, unfragmented analysis of man's nature and his capabilities as well as the requirements of an orderly, effectively functioning society.

Regarding Television

We see television as a powerful social force, an informative, values-reenforcing, ideas-giving medium, with recreational and escapist possibilities.

We distinguish between the actual and the fictional or formula-fitting, "stylized," portrayals of violence. We believe that the two have different probable effects. We are inclined to hold that the more closely the viewer perceives the television picture as portraying a real situation, the more likely it is to affect his attitudes and behavior.

As we seek to distinguish between the actual and the fictional we seek criteria to guide such distinctions. Concerning the reporting of actual events, we stress the need for representative accuracy, and for balancing the importance of the right of public access to information against the dangers of possibly inflaming the issue in conflict and of invading the privacy of the persons involved. In any fictionalized or formula-fitting (stylized) programs, we underscore the need for the sense of proportion, in relation both to other programming and to life as a whole. We highlight the urgency of developing portrayals of other responses to injustice and frustration, and of ways of handling conflict more positively than through the violence situations usually portrayed. Our goal in urging this is not to protect people from reality, but to avoid one-sided distortions of reality.

We accept the general assumption that television has a significant effect on the attitudes and behavior of persons. We believe that this effect is so subtle and indirect that currently available research methodology cannot precisely measure its impact. We know, of course, that television is not the only influencer of personal attitudes and behavior. We sense that it is the response of some trusted person who helps interpret what is seen and heard that becomes a significant factor, particularly for the child. From our understanding of current research findings we agree that television violence may have a mixed effect, with either constructive or destructive consequences. It may prompt corrective action to end the injustices which bred the violence. But sometimes, as the National Commission on Violence concluded, "Violence on television encourages violent forms of behavior, and fosters moral and social values about violence in daily life which are unacceptable in a civilized society." Neither categorical rejection nor endorsement of violence on television appears to be a valid response.

We underscore the need for more research, done under a variety of auspices, which will provide more accurate information on the effects of television viewing upon personal attitudes, personal behavior, and the prevailing social climate. Meanwhile, we believe that constructive action is needed now, and that such constructive action must take place on the basis of currently-informed judgment, credible hypotheses, and the best-available evidence presently at hand.

Whatever our judgments on the effects of television, we recognize that there are many in the broadcasting industry who are doing all they can to serve both the expressed desires of viewers and the genuine public interest. These constructive elements want to see television used to its optimum social potential, not abused either for narrow self-interest, the degradation of persons or groups, or the destruction of society. Such constructive elements, represented especially in leadership persons, we believe require our support, encouragement, and commendation.

Television, however, operates in the public domain. Society cannot rely for its control solely on the good intentions of those in the television industry. Therefore, the many interests, elements, and organizations in society need to be involved in clarifying the goals and objectives, defining the standards, and watching over the performance of television. We favor the idea of a Citizens' Commission on Television, a National Council on Broadcasting Excellence, or some similar representative body, however it might be constituted, which would have powers to influence the work and decisions of the Congress, the Federal Communications Commission, and the industry.

Regarding Person and Community

We regard the television viewer—the perceiver—as a key. All persons do not perceive the same image on the television screen in the same way. Therefore, all programs do not have the same impact. Somehow we must take the perceiver, his age and maturity, his understanding of reality, and the experiences he brings to his perception, into account before we can evaluate the effects of television. We understand, too, that an important element the perceiver brings from his experiences is his own image and picture of himself as a person, in his own right and in relation to others.

We express our concern for the values which television espouses or portrays. Many persons within The American Lutheran Church react unfavorably to the false standards, the false values, the false images, and the disproportions which television so often portrays. We feel that television furthers many misconceptions and wrong expectations about the realities of life both in its regular programs and in its commercials. We sense that these discrepancies between what is pictured and what is typical, or indeed the differences between *what is* and *what ought to be,* may be productive of violence even though in and of themselves they picture no violence.

We agree that family and group viewing (particularly group viewing under congregational auspices), and the resultant discussions, evaluation, and discriminating valuation of television, need to be fostered. We see the study of various sources of advance information regarding television programming as being an essential tool in this task. We encourage the use of existing sources of information, such as *Saturday Review, TV Guide,* and the Television Information Office, toward this goal. We strongly encourage turning sets off and leaving them off when there is no program which merits viewing. Children especially need this evidence of disciplined viewing; television ought not be made into a babysitter. We urge expressions of appreciation to broadcasters and sponsors for responsible programming.

Regarding the Church
In Its Approach to Television as a Social Force

The church needs to remember and build upon its mediating, reconciling role. Cutting across all groups in society, it can have a positive healing influence unlike that of any other organization. It has a prophetic role, which is an essential aspect of its role as servant of the living Lord. In this spirit we purpose that the Church Council take action to:

a. Encourage study throughout the districts, conferences, and parishes of The American Lutheran Church, of the broad theological, psychological, and sociological implications of "the climate of violence" which is widely assumed to be growing in intensity in contemporary society. Such study should enlist competent scholars and research specialists able to relate existing data and trends to conditions as they prevail, community by community, and to stimulate interest, concern, and responsible action on the part of church members.

b. Encourage study, at all appropriate levels, of television as a social force capable through its programming of exerting immeasurable influence upon society. Such study should take into account the relative potential of various styles and forms of program content (fictional drama, fantasy, factual documentary, news, music, etc.), relating each to its positive or negative potential in the various categories of probable audiences.

c. Encourage members of The American Lutheran Church to avail themselves of such documentary specials, outstanding motion pictures, and other significant television programming as are found to be stimulating, informative, and educational; to the end that

(1) families be admonished to give guidance and leadership to home exposure to television fare, rather than permitting happenstance, unsupervised viewing of whatever may be offered;

(2) small group discussion sessions be encouraged to arrange for planned participation and mutual sharing under local parish auspices;

(3) available sources of advance programming information be publicized for planned utilization by parish group leaders; and

(4) church members be encouraged to build responsive relationships with local television managements, either in appreciation for wholesome programming, or in constructive criticism where warranted.

d. Express appreciation on behalf of The American Lutheran Church to television network officials, and other leaders of the industry at the national level, for their efforts to provide wholesome program materials for their massive audiences, to reduce the portrayals of violence in television programming and to strip such portrayals of their glamour, and to develop more stringent self-regulatory codes in the best interests of general audience viewing.

e. Encourage representatives of the national television industry to undertake creative new production enterprises designed to enrich program content for whole family viewing, for children's viewing and possible viewing by other specialized audiences on appropriate time schedules not necessarily identical with present scheduling concepts.

f. Encourage the television industry at the national level to expand its research and to encourage other independent research into the social and psychological effectiveness of its output.

g. Approve in principle current public efforts to establish a strong national commission, council, or agency representative of major segments of the general public for the purpose of effectively safeguarding the basic rights, interests, and concerns of the American public, such a body to be so constituted as to be capable of exerting influence upon Congress, the Federal Communications Commission, and the television industry.

B. THE ENVIRONMENTAL CRISIS

On recommendation of the Commission on Research and Social Action and the Church Council the 1970 Convention adopted the following statement as "expressing the judgment and corporate conviction of The American Lutheran Church as its contribution to the discussions seeking an informed solution to a difficult problem of contemporary life and society."

The rapid deterioration of the natural environment has become a matter of great concern for many Americans. Scientists tell us that we have only a few decades before many of our air, water, and land resources are polluted to a point of no return. Both mass media coverage and statements by government officials have made concern about the quality of our environment a major national issue. Citizens individually and in groups have become aroused about the possible ill effects of air and water pollution, the use of pesticides, and the production and use of nuclear energy. Concern is expressed whether the supply of such natural resources as minerals, forests, agricultural land, and outdoor recreational areas will continue to meet growing population and industrial demands.

The issues raised by concern for the environment among government, business, industry, and individual citizens are enormously complex. Ecologists (who study the relationship of organisms to their environment) have shown how every human decision affects the complex web of relationships that sustains natural processes. Policy decisions about our use of natural resources reflect the basic values by which our civilization lives. As Christians, therefore, we are concerned to participate in discussions and decisions about the human use of the earth in ways that reflect our Christian faith and values.

The Roots of the Environmental Crisis

The dramatic growth of human population has placed enormous pressure upon the physical environment. It took thousands of years for human population to reach one billion around 1850. By 1960 it reached three and a half billion. At the present rate of increase the earth's human population will double in the next 30 years! Population growth was a natural way of aiding the survival of earlier human society. But questions now arise: how many people can the earth sustain? How can we provide the physical and cultural needs, and handle the waste products, of billions of people without destroying the natural environment? Do people have a natural right to produce as many children as they wish? Such questions force a basic policy decision upon the nations of the world: Shall they rely on natural processes to curb, or technological advances to cope with, the rapid growth of population? Or shall it be a matter of public policy to control population growth? What forms of population control can be effective without destroying basic human and democratic rights and values?

The equally dramatic growth of human technology places additional burdens on the earth's carrying capacity. Environmental deterioration is evident not only in overpopulated areas but also in areas of lesser population with a highly developed technology. Modern technology has opened exciting new possibilities for the elimination of drudgery, the widening of man's capabilities and horizons, and for increased control over disease and hunger. But in affluent countries, each person places great material and energy demands on available resources. New agricultural and industrial technologies, in addition to promising new benefits, may also create forms of pollution and undesirable side-effects, which we cannot yet handle. This poses the questions: Shall new technologies be put into use before their probable effects on the environment are determined? To what extent can man continue to use the earth as a technological laboratory?

Our use of technology is determined by the basic values and goals we seek in our society. Technology can be used to husband the resources of the earth or to exploit them for material gain.

Technological and economic development may be necessary for underdeveloped countries intent on raising substandard living conditions. But just as population growth can reach a point where it becomes a threat to national survival, so the continued economic growth and exploitation of resources by affluent countries raises serious questions about national priorities. How much material accumulation is necessary for the good life? At what points may it become necessary to slow economic growth? Upon whom should the burden of such a slowdown fall? Are we willing to set limits to our consumption of materials if the health of our total environment requires it? How can we recycle the waste materials of our present economy to reduce pollution and preserve resources?

Another contributor to the environmental crisis is the fragmentation of political and economic decision-making processes. The specialization of science and technology; the arbitrary geography of political units; the self-interest drives of political and economic units all contribute to making it difficult to establish and enforce policies that conserve the total human and natural environment. It is difficult to achieve the "ecological vision" of the whole web of life. Where will the tools be found to effect the vision? What new forms of political and economic decision making will be needed to create an "ecological" politics?

Problems of Cleaning Up the Environment

Answers to such central questions are needed if mankind genuinely seeks to restore the quality of the environment. The search for such answers will raise many questions about implementation. Some questions will require scientific and technical competence. But other policy questions require decisions by concerned citizens based on social considerations and value judgments:

a. Who decides what our national policy shall be? Do we need statements of overall environmental policy and priorities by our national and state governments? Should such goals be set by administrative agencies, citizens' commissions, legislative action, or constitutional amendments? What is the role of the federal government in setting standards or in financing projects? What should be left to state and local governments? Are new forms of regional agencies such as watershed districts needed?

b. What are our priorities? Though choices are rarely clear-cut, we will have to indicate priorities on a host of difficult questions. For example: Will we insist on air and water pollution standards if they cost us some industrial development and jobs? Are we willing to set some controls on use of automobiles, which are a major source of air pollution?

What controls do we want on use of pesticides and herbicides which may increase agricultural production to feed and clothe growing populations? Shall some remaining wild areas be designated for wilderness preservation, recreational use, or multiple use? How much weight will we give to preserving natural beauty or wildlife if these are threatened by industrial or housing developments?

c. Who pays? Estimates vary widely, but all economists agree that cleaning up present forms of pollution will cost billions of dollars. The American citizen will ultimately bear the cost, either in higher taxes and prices for cleaning up pollution, or else in health costs and other "hidden social costs" of putting up with it. But how shall costs be distributed? Shall government subsidize pollution control projects directly, through tax breaks, or by collecting fines on pollutants? Or should it leave costs to individual polluters and those directly affected by their decisions?

d. What is the role of the individual citizen? The environmental crisis calls not only for public policy decisions, but for the reevaluation by every individual of his role as consumer of goods, services, and power, and as a molder of public opinion and values. What changes am I willing to make in my consumption of goods, my use of fuels, my disposal of waste and litter? How can I inform myself on the public issues involved, and on the principles of ecology which underlie them? Citizens' groups have often been in the forefront of the fight to preserve our environment. Which ones should I help? Or what new group may be needed in my community? Am I willing to use the channels of corporate power open to me to speak and act on my convictions? Most basic is the question: what values do I seek? Do I want to help promote a diversity of environments and possible life styles, or reduce the environment to a few patterns? Do I want to husband the resources of our land or use them up in an economy based on quick turnover and planned obsolescence?

The Concern of the Churches

Behind all the questions of political, economic, and scientific policies toward the environment lies a fundamental religious concern: What is man's relationship toward the world which he inhabits? Nature has often been seen as the enemy of man, to be fought and mastered. It has often been seen as an inexhaustible treasure to be plundered. But the very success of man in conquering and exploiting nature now threatens his own welfare and survival. Christians have often participated in and justified the exploitation of nature. But a more careful understanding of Scriptures will lead us to a renewed care for the earth.

As Christians we affirm God's creation. God created all things and proclaimed each thing good, even before man was created. He proclaimed the whole of nature—including man—as "very good" (Genesis 1). Our response to the world God created is properly neither fear nor greed, but respect for and celebration of everything in it as the handiwork of God.

As Christians we witness to Incarnation and Sacrament. Even though man in his fall corrupted himself and subjected nature to bondage, God did not abandon his creation to futility (Romans 8). In Christ he entered our flesh in order to redeem all things; in the common elements of water, bread, and wine he covenants that redemption sacramentally with us. We dare not despise, misuse, or ignore what God created, redeemed, and inhabits, but thankfully live in hope of the redemption of all things.

As Christians we are held responsible to an ethic of stewardship. God's charge to man, "Be fruitful and multiply, and fill the earth and subdue it; and have dominion . . ." (Genesis 1:28), seen in the light of Christian stewardship, is not a charter for human pride and exploitation of nature, but a mandate to be representatives of God in caring for the earth, as he cares for it. In Christ we have the freedom and responsibility to live in ways that reflect that care. Christian stewardship will be reflected, not only in individual styles of life, but in communal concern, as the body of Christ, for the health and welfare of the total environment that we share with all living things.

As a church body we must teach and practice these truths as they relate to maintaining and restoring the quality of our environment. We urge that the entire American Lutheran Church make an intensive study for the next two years of the issues raised by the environmental crisis. The programs of the divisions, commissions, and auxiliaries of the national offices, and the activities of the districts and conferences, should reflect this concern. Congregations should provide opportunities for study and service which help equip their members to act responsibly on the issues involved. Members should especially be encouraged to fulfill their vocational roles in their homes and in their occupations in ways that enhance rather than damage the environment. In its own economic practices each unit of the corporate church needs to be mindful of its responsibilities for the care of the earth. Not only in its word but also in its deeds the whole of Christ's Church should be in the forefront of those who care and act in the environmental crisis.

C. TRAFFIC SAFETY

1968 Convention action: To approve the statement on "Traffic Safety" and that it be "commended to the congregations for study."

The toll in injury, death, and destruction that traffic exacts on American streets and highways should deeply concern The American Lutheran Church. What should especially distress us is that so much of this pain, grief, heartbreak, loss, and destruction is utterly needless. For, as we see it, traffic accidents result in large part from ignorant, thoughtless, careless, rash, impetuous, reckless, or irresponsible behavior.

We teach that Christ expects his followers to lead disciplined, controlled, responsible lives. He calls upon each of his own to govern themselves by the effect of their actions upon other persons. We believe that the fruits of his Spirit—"love, joy, peace, patience, kindness, goodness, faithfulness, gentleness, self control"—are as much in place behind the steering wheel as before the altar.

We believe, too, that effective law and authority are needed to curb dangerous practices and to foster wholesome behavior in traffic. We support sound legislation designed to promote traffic safety. In particular we endorse legislation that will effectively curb the menace of driving under the influence of alcohol or drugs. We uphold that exercise of public authority which enforces such sound legislation with honor, justice, integrity, consistency, and impartiality.

Many other groups beyond the legislative and the enforcement agencies also must be mobilized in the fight for traffic safety. We urge particularly that those with commercial interests at stake— automobile manufacturers and dealers, petroleum and rubber industries, service station and repair businesses, truck and bus operators, contractors for street and highway construction, beverage alcohol venders, and insurance underwriters, for example—marshal their resources for a coordinated attack on the evils that imperil our traffic on streets and highways.

Members of The American Lutheran Church should support informed, decisive, and constructive action toward improving traffic safety. Such action needs to move simultaneously on many fronts, which will seek to:

a. engineer maximum safety features into streets and highways, signs and markers, road surfaces, and access to highways, including the setting of realistic speed limits;

b. design motor vehicles to insure safety, to foster comfort, and to guard against foreseeable contingencies;

c. train and screen drivers more thoroughly in order to weed out the incompetent, irresponsible, or error-prone;

d. educate pedestrians to avoid thoughtless and hazardous actions and to keep from bringing upon an innocent driver the anguish of a pedestrian accident he could not prevent;

e. improve legislative, enforcement, and judicial controls so as to win and maintain citizen respect for just laws and for their fair and impartial administration;

f. expand research efforts to provide valid answers to questions basic to the broad scope of traffic safety;

g. provide increased funding for public and private agencies, through both taxes and voluntary contributions, necessary to finance a comprehensive attack on traffic evils;

h. develop an enlightened public opinion which will give the tone, dimension, and support needed to effect responsible programs for traffic safety.

Traffic safety starts with each driver and each pedestrian. The American Lutheran Church urges each of its members to take to heart and to put into practice these points of personal action for traffic safety:

a. Know and obey all laws for drivers and pedestrians;

b. Use available safety devices, such as seat belts;

c. Keep yourself and your car in error-free control;

d. Avoid compulsive driving under such emotional conditions as anger, hostility, depression, or exhilaration;

e. Stay alert for the other person's error;

f. Practice the "Golden Rule" in all situations;

g. Never drive when drugs or alcoholic beverages may impair your abilities;

h. Ride only with a driver you know to be competent and law-abiding;

i. Inform yourself about and support sound proposals for improving traffic safety;

j. Influence others to support effective programs of engineering, education, and enforcement;

k. Express to public officials your opinion on needed measures to improve traffic safety;

l. Accept willingly your share of the financial costs of realistic programs for traffic safety;

m. Pray daily for God's protection upon you and others who use the streets and highways and for his guidance to those who must seek sound solutions for the problems of traffic safety.

D. COMMUNITY COMMUNICATIONS SYSTEMS

The 1968 Convention requested that Dr. Loren Halvorson's observations concerning a community communications systems be included in Reports and Actions of the Convention. *The observations of Dr. Halvorson, at that time assistant director for research and development of the Board of College Education, follow:*

Before a human community can be planned and established, a communications system must be created. This requires:

An Opened Society. A climate is needed which encourages citizens to face each other honestly and openly on devisive issues. A type of dialogue must be achieved which combines a realistic approach to hard issues with an atmosphere of mutual trust.

Civil Courage. At least a few persons are needed in each community so committed to dialogue as to experiment, to raise controversial issues, to insist on honoring diverse points of view and to resist permanent polarization. This new breed of citizenry must be suited for the rich diversity of a pluralistic society, unafraid of controversy and committed to healing action.

Community Partnership. A coalition representing the fullest spectrum of the community is required to provide the common platform for dialogue and action. This coalition must be built on respect for all the participating groups, it must honor the integrity of each partner and must actively provoke or evoke each to fulfill its indivisible responsibility.

Personal Involvement. The one single problem which cuts across all groups, especially those who feel themselves pushed to the community's periphery, is the profound sense of "powerlessness." A communications system is needed with effective feedback so that the invisible, silent, forgotten, and ignored may have a personal sense of involvement. Such an inclusive system does not now exist. It must be built.

Hope. The intensive bombardment of the citizenry with social crises threatens to turn them off and to increase their hostility and frustration. What is needed now, when people are asking, "What can we do?", are examples of demonstrated possibilities, case studies, acts of civil courage revealing how some citizens are dealing realistically and creatively with community problems.

Shared Goals. Procedures must be developed to determine the specific goals for a community which then provide the program agenda for its communications system. This requires study, research, wide-spread citizen participation, community dialogue, and specific actions.

The Communications System should have a definite goal:

To Change People's Attitudes. Toward others, toward themselves, toward issues, and toward the future. The alleged breakdown of American society can be the breaking open of people, institutions, and groups to new relationships and possibilities. Our society must be persuaded that the future is still open and in the hands of the citizenry if they act.

To Evoke and Provoke the Nation to Responsible Action. The purpose must be to move people beyond talk to creative action by confronting them with both the issues and the practical and innovative solutions now emerging in our society.

E. AGRICULTURE

The Grape Controversy

By specific request of the president of the church, the Commission on Research and Social Action in early 1969 prepared a statement on issues in the then-current grape boycott. The Church Council in June 1969 approved the following statement "for study and discussion in the congregations of The American Lutheran Church."

Admittedly the "Grape Strike" in Delano, the boycott of California table grapes in selected market areas, the relations between the growers and their workers, and the resultant activities of some churches and church-related groups are intensely emotional issues. Without firsthand, on-the-scene research, one despairs of obtaining precise, objective, trustworthy data. Materials and reports prepared to substantiate the competing viewpoints suggest that alleged facts and statistics are selectively chosen so as to document a predetermined position. In an effort to cut through such self-serving tactics and to identify the underlying issues the Commission on Research and Social Action offers the following analysis as a means for stimulating thinking and promoting discussion within The American Lutheran Church. This analysis represents the commission's acquaintance with the issues through recurrent on-the-scene observations by a staff representative and through careful study of pertinent publications.

While the grape controversy centers in California conditions, similar outcroppings of a farm worker movement have appeared elsewhere, particularly in Texas with the melon harvest. Both in California and in Texas the central issue is the labor organization of farm workers. In California the struggle is over the recognition of the United Farm Workers Organizing Committee (UFWOC), or groups of similar title and intent, as the bargaining agent for farm workers. The workers predominantly are Mexican-American in background, in the process of making a transition from a migratory to a more settled way of life. Though the quoted hourly wage suggests that the workers receive an adequate pay, it must be recalled that for many laborers their farm work is seasonal and spasmodic. Thus their annual earnings are quite inadequate in comparison with the earnings of typical American workers in other industries. The conditions under which farm labor is done, especially on corporation farms, give rise to labor unrest. At peak periods the laborer is indispensable; at other periods he is expendable and is regarded by some as a drain on the community's resources. The laboring conditions, complicated by problems of housing, education, and medical care, and combined with the struggle for recognition of human dignity, underlie efforts to organize workers to improve conditions regarded as undesirable. Some church groups have associated themselves with this cause, which they define as morally just and right.

The widespread publicity surrounding the California situation, interpreted in so many different ways, has popularized the terms "Grape Strike" and "Grape Boycott." It also has highlighted "La Raza," "the movement" to gain and wield "Brown Power." Nevertheless, the conflict in the San Joaquin Valley may well prove to be the leading edge of a farm labor movement which will eventually affect most farmers and farm workers in the United States, whether their produce be fruit, grain, vegetables, livestock, or poultry. The California situation illuminates the fact that agribusiness*— not the family farm or the small grower—is the dominant power in late 20th century agriculture. While much understandable sympathy focuses on the plight of the small grower in the California conflict, there are strong indications that it is corporation farming, agribusiness, and changing agricultural technology—not the labor organization efforts of farm workers—which are squeezing the small grower out of agriculture. This is not to suggest that the grape strike leaves him unaffected; indeed it likely will work a severe hardship on the small grower, perhaps even being the proverbial "straw that broke the camel's back." Yet, the deeper, underlying factors are the changing economic scene, concentrations of economic power and capital, the inability of the grower to set the selling price for his product, complex technology requiring ever-larger

---

* Agribusiness is a term symbolizing the interlocking of interests in the various stages of agricultural production and marketing, as well as the impersonal aspects of extensive corporate farms.

investments, and the dominance of agribusiness itself which are the greatest threats to the small producer.

Perhaps the most controversial feature of the California conflict is the attempted boycott of table grapes in selected marketing areas, both in the United States and overseas (e.g., Sweden). The boycott is a frequently-used and commonly-accepted tactical tool in economic disputes, intended to bring group pressure to bear in the collective bargaining processes. The boycott of selected labels of wines and spirits was effective in winning recognition of the UFWOC as collective bargaining agent for the workers of such large firms as Schenley, Di Giorgio, Perelli-Minetti, and the Christian Brothers. A similar selective boycott of table grapes marketed under particular labels was the original intent of UFWOC. However, this intent was thwarted by the rapid switching of marketing labels by a number of large growers. Consequently, the UFWOC extended its boycott across the board to all California-grown table grapes, and requested the support of all organized labor in its move. Again, this is a usual, not an unusual, tactic to gain recognition for a specific goal of organized labor. Wherever used it arouses either sympathy or outrage. The present situation is no exception to this rule.

The current boycott of table grapes has been a pressure device for gaining recognition for the farm workers' cause. It also has worked some hardships upon the growers of such grapes, especially upon the smaller growers who may be heavily mortgaged in their operations, who lack the protection of tax havens or tax write-offs, who need the income from their crop and have neither the storage facilities nor working capital to withhold their product from market until prices are more favorable, and who in other ways do not enjoy the economic power of the large growers. There are many parallels to the current California situation in the bitter record of the efforts of industrial workers to organize for collective bargaining in the 1930s and of trade unions and craftsmen to organize in the late nineteenth and early twentieth centuries. The protests against "outside agitators," "Red influence," and "the economic impossibility of meeting workers' demands," for example, ring a familiar tone. The protections which the farm workers seek are essentially those already won by industrial laborers over three decades ago. The locale now, though, is not factories with smokestacks but "factories in the fields."

For the church the central question does not revolve around the legitimacy of the boycott as a tool of organized labor, or the right of farm workers to organize for collective bargaining and protection of their legitimate interests. These are tactics and goals accepted in other areas of society. The central question is the plight of the persons involved and effective ways of bringing justice to bear on their situation. This raises for the church the practical question of the necessity, propriety, or wisdom of the church as a corporate body in making any statement which appears to favor the bargaining position of either side. This presents a delicate situation, since each side invokes claims of justice, equity, and concern for the total well-being of persons and community. Whatever official statement the corporate church may make is subject to a variety of interpretations, applications, and uses. On the other hand, the church, as the people of God at work in the world, must act on such social issues as conscience compels and wisdom directs. The freedom of the informed and sensitive conscience to respond in word and in deed needs both to be prompted and to be respected in any statement of any church body or church-related group.

The grape strike and boycott are complex, controversial, and emotional. They are symptoms of a deeper struggle over the shape and conduct of American agriculture. That there are ethical issues, with Christian implications, in the labor-management struggle going on in the vineyards of California we do not doubt. They cannot be debated in isolation, however, from the deeper economic struggle of competing forces. The task of the church in this situation is to minister meaningfully to all parties in the struggle. It needs to provide a reconciling forum where persons of divergent views can express their opinions frankly and openly and can hear the frank and open views of others who disagree. As a channel for open expression and honest acceptance of people where they are and where they can be helped, by the grace of God, to move, the church can be a healing influence for civic justice.

It is our belief that the constructive efforts necessary for civic justice and reconciliation among those involved in the grape controversy supersede the issues of the boycott itself. Regardless of the views which Christians may hold on the boycott, we encourage members of the ALC, especially but not only those in California, to support efforts to bring about needed changes in the basic conditions which give rise to the current controversy. We respect the integrity of judgment of informed members of the ALC to act as the Spirit gives them wisdom and as their circles of opportunity permit.

With respect to the workers, we favor: (1) legal recognition of the right of farm workers to organize and to bargain collectively under the protections of appropriate federal legislation; (2) educational and retraining opportunities for farm workers to equip them for other agricultural or for non-agricultural employment; and (3) advocacy assistance to them in their participation in the economic, social, and political communities in which they live or work.

In efforts to deal with the plight of the small growers, we favor: (1) wider recognition of major changes in agricultural technology and the size of economic units, including the possibility of expanding the cooperative movement among small growers; (2) tax reforms which end preferential protections to certain types of farm owners not directly or primarily involved in agricultural production; and (3) legal recognition of efforts by the growers to set fair and equitable prices for agricultural commodities which compensate the producers justly for their time, management skills, and capital investment.

Such measures, we believe, will help to foster the civic justice and reconciliation for which the church stands. Support of church members for such measures will indicate in action the meaning of "the more abundant life" (see John 10:10) which God offers to all men. Advocacy of such measures for the benefit of workers and growers is a concrete way by which Christians can help to make known to all men the lordship of Jesus Christ.

Rural Economic Problems

On assignment from the 1968 General Convention the Commission on Research and Social Action in 1969 developed a statement on this topic. Acting on the 1970 Church Council recommendation the 1970 Convention approved it "as a statement of comment and counsel addressed to members of The American Lutheran Church to aid them in their decisions and actions."

A Perspective on the Whole Scene

The rural America of nostalgic memory is gone. The adoption and use of technology destroyed it. A renewed rural America is emerging, reshaped in character, outlook, and way of life. Technology is the tool rebuilding rural America. It is a force that has been welcomed by those using it, often without realizing its far-reaching consequences. The massive changes rural America is experiencing—stemming from its acceptance of technology—are revolutionary in their impact. They are as crucial for America—though neither as visible nor as audible—as are the crises in the cities. Indeed, many a refugee displaced by the rural revolution quietly flees to the cities, in this way contributing to the urban discontent. On the other hand, some former urban dwellers are moving into rural America, with their urban experiences and urban expectations.

Such massive changes—alike in nonrural as in rural areas—bring problems. They bring problems to persons, to families, to the communities around which people's lives revolve, and to the institutions and agencies of rural America, including the church. They bring problems of job opportunities, of mobility, of housing, of health and medical care, of education, of government, of recreation and leisure time, of trade and commerce, of religious leadership, etc. They bring problems of land use and management, of pricing and marketing, of production and distribution, of financing, and of weighing the claims of the competing farm organizations. Such massive changes raise issues of poverty and dependency, of power and powerlessness, of governmental versus voluntary action, of ways of controlling change toward desired ends, and of the role of the church in the community.

Rural economic problems need to be viewed in some such broad perspective. The current crop of rural economic problems results from the fact and the consequences of technology. The problems reflect a clash between different sets of values and expectations about *what-is* and *what-ought-to-be*. They require the development of workable policies fair and equitable to all parties affected by them. They necessitate review of how such resources as land, labor, machinery, and working capital are allocated among the possible claims for their use. Efforts to solve rural economic problems, based on accurate analyses, revolve around a sensitive implementation of wise decisions.

Effects of Technology

Technology, as a tool, is neither good nor evil in itself. Applied to rural America, technology has added far more assets than liabilities. Few farmers would want to return to the pretechnological era of farming prior to 1935. The nation needs the technological efficiency of its agriculture, which now permits one American farmer to produce the food and fiber needed by 43 persons. Despite the costs and consequences of technology for persons and communities, few persons seriously argue for a retreat to 1935. Rather, the call is for renewal. The need is to use technology—with its chemicals, machinery, automation, and applications of science to agriculture—toward its optimum social feasibility.

An ironic twist resulting from technology affects farmers. Farmers tend to think of themselves as both employer and employee, yet are frustrated in securing some of the advantages believed to attach to each role. Farmers are compensated as industry, not as labor. Though the farmer is an entrepreneur, he cannot effectively price his goods to compensate him at prevailing rates for his capitalization costs and his management skills. He operates with some of the disadvantages of unorganized labor. The number of farmers selling their products is large, but the number of direct purchasers able to buy their products is small. Hence, unless farmers organize to control the marketing of their product, they are at the mercy of the few available buyers.

Technology also has changed the size, shape, functions, and relationships of the rural community. The time/distance factor by which people are willing to decide how far they will go to obtain goods and services has been influenced by the automobile, improved roads, the telephone, and other media of transportation and communication. In the competition some rural trade centers are losing, others are gaining. No one center alone has a near monopoly. People may shop for groceries or bank in one center, for an automobile in another, obtain health care or legal services in a third community, buy their dress clothes in a fourth center, and seek recreational outlets in yet another community. The mobility which technology permits has given rural people a far greater freedom of choice than they previously enjoyed.

Value Systems in Competition

The farmer traditionally is a rugged individualist, proud of his freedom to operate as he chooses. Today, however, he is learning the urgency of cooperation. He may cooperate voluntarily through participation in farm organizations and movements, or under the compulsion of government regulations. Joint action, he is learning, is essential to his economic success, to the health of his community, and to his responsible participation in American life. The Christian farmer is seeing that cooperative action is a way of expressing love for neighbor as for self.

Rural America shares values widespread in American life. These stress economic efficiency, success, narrow specialization and a concentration on one's specialty, money-making, indulgence in gadgets and things, and a desire for "a better life" for one's children. Yet many of these operating values contradict the nobler values held up as characteristic of America at its best. This contradiction between what is professed and what is practiced stirs a current revolt by sensitive youth.

Values to which rural America, indeed all America, should give priority attention include justice and equity, equality of opportunity, compassion, opportunity for creative diversity, and a wise use and management of resources, all of which represent obedience to God. They include also an appreciation for family relationships, leisure and recreation, the capacity to enjoy life and the beautiful things of life, the opportunities to serve other persons and the interests of others, and the possibilities inherent in participation in the work and fellowship of groups and organizations. Such values include a high quality of life within the community. An enjoyable community is marked by sensitivity to spiritual considerations, adequate housing, good government, relevant education, reasonably available health care, recreational facilities and gathering places for leisure time activities, accurately reliable communication facilities, an aesthetic blending and use of spatial considerations, concern for the disadvantaged and powerless, and citizen participation in projects and activities that advance the interests of the community as a whole.

Such values are communicated in words, in practice, and within relationships. Residents of rural America need consciously to express in their personal lives and in their communities the positive values which emphasize the considerate rather than the aggressive nature of man.

Policies Expressive of Values

Public policies reflect whatever consensus there may be on values which should be incorporated into actions. In this sense, Christians should commend measures, related to rural economic problems, which:

a. Foster the size of a farming operation which is commensurate with the requirements of modern farming in a specific geographic area;

b. Encourage informed and responsible use of cooperative action to promote the well-being of rural people and their communities;

c. Stress attainment of the economic well-being of farm people in relation to other segments of society;

d. Deal constructively with the eroding forces of rural poverty, widespread, diffuse, lonely, and unnoticed in its hunger and its hopelessness;

e. Establish equitable tax policies, correcting the injustices inherent in an ineffective use of the property tax and in various "tax loopholes";

f. Provide feasible ways of helping people economically to remain in rural areas, if they wish, rather than allowing economic pressures alone to force them out of the rural community;

g. Build bridges of education, expand vocational training and retraining, and provide rehabilitation for persons displaced from agriculture, undergirded by a compassionate awareness of and sensitivity to their difficulties;

h. Enhance opportunities for the fulfillment of personality, permitting the person to realize the maximum of satisfactions in his own life and his relations with others;

i. Conserve and improve the resources of soil, air, and water in stewardship of God's grant of dominion over the earth, making prudent allocations of time, energy, and funds in this total resource management;

j. Seek to manage and control the dynamic forces of change into directions accepted as wholesome and salutary for the best interests of all parties involved;

k. Prevent harm and distress to people and communities by taking positive action in counseling, welfare, and health services to avoid problems or to correct them before they intensify;

l. Protect personal and institutional integrity by encouraging the exchange of ideas and of practices, thus opening various options and enlarging the range of freedom for responsible choice and action; and

m. Assist communities, alone and in combination, to cope with greed and avarice, to attack their own problems, and to work out their own approaches for insuring a more livable community.

Reallocation of Community Resources

The conclusion is inescapable that *given current conditions* rural America is marked by over-capacity and under-attractiveness. Farmers can supply more food and fiber than present demands can absorb. There are more farmers than modern farming techniques require. More churches, more schools, more governmental units, more trading centers dot the rural scene than are needed under current conditions. Youth leave their rural homes for opportunities elsewhere. Yet, doctors, dentists, lawyers, teachers, clergymen, and others willing to work in rural America are in short supply. Dealing with the institutional and service imbalance in rural areas, on the basis of the new technology, is essential for improving the quality of living in rural America.

Clearly, a critical review of the ways in which communities allocate their resources of people and dollars is in order. Community development and rural area development are needed steps in this process. Such processes require (a) systematic discussion to determine the needs felt by the people and the intensity of their feelings; (b) a systematic plan to carry out the first self-help projects that the people have agreed upon, depending upon local leaders to get the task done; (c) a mobilization and harnessing of the physical, economic, and social potential of all the groups in the community, relying heavily upon trusted media of communication; and (d) creation of a climate of aspiration on the part of the people of the community to undertake improvement projects they have agreed are needed, and of confidence that success is possible because the entire community has decided to work together in a common cause. The rigid independence of yesterday's rural communities will give way to the flexible partnership of tomorrow's. In the process some of today's smaller towns will find they no longer need to be complete communities. They can find their new life and place as partners in a larger community, with an economic base, social institutions, and supporting services, all tied together by networks of transportation and communication. Each partner, as a member of the whole, will contribute in its own dynamic way to the strength of the flexible community of the future.

Exactly what reallocations of resources will be realistic and realizable will become clear in the development process. Skilled resource persons, competent in various areas of specialization, need to be enlisted for help in the processes of community development. Such persons are on the staffs of federal and state governmental agencies, colleges and universities, trade and professional associations, and church organizations, among others. Their expertise is essential, to help cut through the narrow self-interest which so often mars efforts to reallocate community resources.

Role and Opportunities for the Church

The influence of the organized church in coping with rural economic problems is primarily an indirect one, inherent in its role of "discipling" (see Matt. 28:19, 20), "enabling" (see 1 Tim. 1:12), and "equipping" (see Eph. 4:11-13). Its secondary role, as an institution, is to make its own changes in structures and operations so as to be effective in mission under current conditions.

Many persons in rural America suffer an identity crisis, not sure of their own worth or standing on the social scale. Fear and frustration may make them apathetic or hostile. To such a situation the church can speak a freeing, forgiving, vision-raising word about man as God sees him. The church can concentrate less on where man is and to what depths he has fallen, by showing instead what man can become and what destiny God desires for man.

In ministering to a changing rural America, the church needs to help its people cope with change. It needs to help them distinguish between the wholesome and the destructive aspects of change. It needs to motivate its people to support the positive thrusts and to counteract the negative sides of change. The church needs to help its people accept the fact that living amid the realities of change is one of the facts of life. It is in the processes of positive change that the Christian should see the goodness of the creation and the continuing evidence of God's gift of grace through life.

As the people of God, the church enrolls countless members with expertise and competence in innumerable fields. One of its key tasks is to motivate, equip, and release these members for their witness and service in the secular structures of rural America. Communities often are starved for persons of leadership stature and ability. The church can enjoin its members to fill such roles of community service, to inject needed vision and enthusiasm into the community, and to exemplify in their lives the high values which rural America should espouse.

The better to equip its members for their service in community, the church should provide direct opportunities for confronting and informing them on key problems. Information and ideas should be exposed, creative and innovative possibilities explored, and optional lines of action opened. The church needs to remain alert to its information-sharing, conscience-pricking, and response-stimulating roles in the community.

Stewardship is both a concept and a way of life for the Christian. The implications of stewardship for the conservation, management, and allocation or reallocation of resources are a part of the message of the church for rural America. In this process the church, its pastors and congregations, will want to keep in touch with, and make use of, the programs and services of governmental and other agencies operating in rural America.

Institutionally the church needs to make adjustments in light of current problems in rural America. It needs to:

a. Foster in a creative way the realignment of congregations for more effective ministry in rural areas, involving the affected congregations in the decision-making processes;

b. Recognize the difficulties in transferring loyalties from one established and interlocking web of relationships to another;

c. Train persons in (1) the skills of counseling to help congregations reach wise decisions, and (2) the arts of interpersonal relations to bring about a broader, popularly based involvement in corporate planning and action;

d. Adapt the lessons learned in the cooperative movement, in medical and health care services, in business and education circles, and others, to its own structures and operations, especially in their approaches to team ministry and cluster-communities;

e. Prepare its pastors, as enablers and equippers of their people, to deal in an understanding way with the issues of rural economic problems, the research that illumines these problems, the effects these problems have on people and families, and the recognition of diversities and individual differences which both complicate and aid the correction of these problems;

f. Tell more widely the story of what the church is doing, the mutual cooperation and helpfulness it engenders, the congregations which have gracefully completed their life span, the renewed congregations which have helped to reshape their communities, the sharing of surpluses in money, leadership, people, and ideas among congregations, the sensitivity of the church to social reality, and the "pastoral improvement seminars" and continuing education opportunities it offers its pastors.

Rural economic problems affect the whole of rural life. Since they are economic in origin, any corrective action must include sound economic components. Since these problems are part of the whole of rural life, any corrective action cannot be solely economic. It must include social, psychological, educational, and political components. Above all, it must address itself to the spirit of man, created in the image and likeness of God (Gen. 1:26), a creature whose reflected glory Psalm 8 pictures in poetic language. From its Biblical perspective on man and his life in all of its relationships the church has an intense interest in rural economic problems. It calls for man to use the benefits of technology to renew and rebuild rural America. The church keynotes the need for sound values, equitable policies, strategic allocation of resources, and resolute implementation of wise decisions in this application of technology to the renewal and rebuilding of rural America. The church, as the servant of the living Lord, gladly associates itself with this complex and herculean task. It does so in the spirit of 2 Tim. 1:7: "for God did not give us a spirit of timidity but a spirit of power and love and self-control."

Bargaining Power for Farmers

In acting on an assignment from the 1968 Convention for a statement on this topic, the Commission on Research and Social Action requested one of its members, Dr. H. B. Sorensen, associate professor in the department of agricultural economics and sociology at Texas A. and M. University to prepare the statement. The following statement, written and revised by Dr. Sorensen in light of responses received to earlier drafts, was adopted by the 1970 Convention as "a statement of comment and counsel addressed to members of The American Lutheran Church to aid them in their decisions and actions."

The Commission on Research and Social Action of The American Lutheran Church was asked by the 1968 General Convention to explore the issues involved in collective bargaining for farmers. The current situation wherein over ninety percent of American people are living in towns, cities, and suburbs, and wherein controversy has attached to such activities as governmental farm programs, the National Farmers Organization holding action, and the California Grape Boycott at the retail store level, makes an analysis and clear understanding of the possibilities of collective bargaining imperative.

The Cooperative Approach

Individual farmers, like individual laborers, control too small a proportion of their total supply to bargain effectively like the labor unions in the automobile industry, for example. Therefore a cooperative bargaining association may be organized to represent many farmers.

A cooperative is a business voluntarily owned and controlled by its member-patrons and operated for them on a nonprofit or cost basis. More specifically it is a business organization, usually incorporated, owned, and controlled by members or stock holders, as producers or patrons on a cost basis after allowing for expenses of the operation and maintenance, and other authorized deductions for expansion and necessary reserves.

The Capper-Volstead Act, passed by Congress, February 1922, states that:

Persons engaged in the production of agricultural products as farmers, planters, ranchmen, dairymen, nut or fruit growers may act together in associations, corporate or otherwise, with or without capital stock, in collectively processing, preparing for market, handling, and marketing in interstate and foreign commerce, such products of persons so engaged. Such associations may have marketing agencies in common; such associations and their members may make the necessary contracts and agreements to effect such purposes: Provided however, That such associations are operated for the mutual benefit of the members thereof, as such producers.

The Bargaining Process

Bargaining is an attempt by an individual or a group to enhance its position relative to those with whom they trade. Bargaining power refers to the ability of a person or group to gain advantageous prices or terms of trade.

Bargaining is not new but is a renewed effort by farmers to gain more favorable terms of trade. It had its American origin with milk producers in New York, as far back as the 1880s. Farmers in California and Utah organized to bargain collectively with fruit and vegetable processors during World War I.

To bargain means to haggle, to negotiate, to compromise while seeking to improve one's position. Bargaining power, then, is the ability to bargain successfully and purposely to bring about improved price and nonprice terms of trade, to achieve advantageous prices and terms of sale through negotiations, to obtain an influentiality in the market place of market power.

A bargaining agreement may be negotiated with the primary handler to pay farmers a higher price, but much of the increase thus gained will be passed on to others in the marketing system.

Collective Bargaining

A collective bargaining association differs from the normal agricultural marketing cooperative in that it usually does not physically handle the products of its members. The function of the association is a bargaining one, without involving the responsibilities of assembling, processing, or distributing the product. The association's bargaining power is derived from its control of adequate quantities of the product.

The major objective of a collective bargaining association is to obtain for its members the highest returns consistent with current and prospective economic conditions and the long term welfare of the growers. Collective bargaining can improve understanding among farmers, handlers, and processors.

Collective bargaining cannot do anymore than what the farmers as a group are willing to have done and to whatever extent they are willing to cooperate in reaching their goals. Collective bargaining cannot change laws of supply and demand; it cannot make a poor product into a high quality product; and it cannot operate just for the other fellow if it is going to be successful. Collective bargaining associations probably offer very limited opportunity for nationally produced storable products such as wheat and corn.

Sources for Possible Gains

Production efficiencies of course are central to any genuine increase in the real income of farmers. In the bargaining processes, however, there are essentially three sources of gain for the farmer: (a) from the profit margins of handlers of the product, (b) from higher prices for products sold to handlers and/or higher prices to consumers, and (c) by increasing market efficiencies through reduced costs.

When farmers talk about bargaining, they usually think of higher prices for the products they sell. The goal of higher prices can be overemphasized. The farmer's real objective is to obtain full market value. Market value is based upon supply, demand, business conditions, trends in usage, imports, and availability and prices of substitutes. Higher prices tend to cause consumers to reduce purchases. The extent of reduced buying depends upon the substitutes available and their prices. Substantially higher prices to producers tend to increase the output. Producer's bargaining power is affected by the political climate, federal and state marketing orders, and agreements or government programs that affect the bargaining environment.

Farmers can get higher prices for their products if consumers pay more, if processors or distributors reduce their margin or profit, or if the handling cost between the farmer and the first receiver of the product is reduced. If the price to consumers is increased, the consumers are more willing or even likely to substitute a lower-priced product—including synthetics—for a higher-priced product.

Gains which may be achieved through collective bargaining action depend on organizational conditions and on the nature of the product. Bargaining gains in the long run must be subject to the limitations of the economic factors peculiar to the product under consideration.

Special Problems for Agriculture

Agricultural production is such that once life is started in either a plant or an animal, it cannot be stopped and started up again as in the automobile industry where car assembly may be stopped and started at any time. If crops are carried to maturity and are harvested, nearly all of them have to go to a market or to a processing plant. Farmers themselves can store only a few of the products they produce. It is difficult to conduct an effective withholding action so long as the farmer has large investments in land, equipment, and livestock. Interest, taxes, and installment payments have to be met, or the farmer is forced out of business. Therefore few farmers can leave their land idle or can afford to withhold their products from the market once they have been produced.

Several conditions have been suggested as necessary to exert enough economic pressure in the bargaining process to achieve gains for farmers. The farmer organization must: (a) represent a sufficient volume of the commodities, (b) have disciplinary power over its members and cohesion among them, (c) obtain recognition by virtue of its ability to exert economic influence, (d) have a membership willing and able to bear the cost of withholding if necessary, and (e) be able to tailor the marketings to demands and get desired prices on a continued basis.

There are two limiting factors encountered that confront most bargaining associations: (a) How much of national production of a product can the bargaining association effectively control? Bargaining associations must control a substantial volume of a product and have an organizational integrity sufficient to command recognition of buyers. (b) Bargaining associations are limited in their ability to enhance prices by the fact that they generally deal with one product (or a limited number of products) and there are many other products which can and do serve as substitutes in consumption.

The Role of Bargaining Associations

Voluntary organizations of producers interested in the same commodity can influence price in terms of trade under certain conditions. They may be able to negotiate a collective bargaining agreement which offers advantages to the buyer through reduced operating cost, with the monetary value of the reduction added to the seller's price. The buyers are assured of a dependable supply and more uniform quality control when dealing with a central agent. Producers may assume certain of the buyer's marketing risks in exchange for increased returns through agreed-upon specifications written into a bargaining agreement.

Some bargaining associations have been successful in representing their growers in collective bargaining action with processors. Farmers in these organizations have, through the use of contracts, passed the control of the sale of their products over to the association. Processors can recognize the association as bargaining agents.

The bargaining associations also have served to increase the uniformity and the mutuality of the contractual relationship between processors and farmers. Use of collective bargaining to force the processing firms to pay a price higher than the competitive supply-demand price has resulted in excessive inventory carryovers. A large inventory carryover always has a depressing effect when it comes to bargaining for the oncoming new crop.

Factors Limiting the Potential

The true potential of collective bargaining lies in these opportunities of the bargaining associations: (a) to provide industry leadership, (b) to provide a method of educating the farmers about relevant factors that determine the price of the product, (c) to expand the demand for farm products through advertising and promotion, (d) to establish a marketing system based on grade and quality, (e) to regulate the flow of the product to market and to offer alternative outlets, and (f) to develop a supply management program based on contracts with buyers.

One source of market power is supply management. There are three methods of managing supplies. *One* is mandatory types of programs administered by the government, which will buy these products from the producers. A *second* approach includes regulations under marketing orders and agreements recommended by producers-shippers and issued by the government. The regulations pertaining to grades, size, maturity, pack, volume, or price are applied to everyone, and producers can tailor the quality, quantity, and the timing of supplies to market requirements better than they can act as a voluntary association. A *third* method is partial supply management which is partly mandatory and includes contract selling through the farmers marketing associations. The most common of these is forward-contracting with delivery price set at contracting time. A less common method is called the participation plan, where the price received by the farmers is not set at contract time but rather is based on the actual selling price of the finished product.

Affecting the Flow to Market

There are three ways to effect the flow of supplies to the market in supply management programs such as those just itemized. (a)

Elimination of some portion of the supply from commercial channels is one method. Elimination means that some part of the production will not be marketed, either now or in the future, regardless of what happens to the price in the future. (b) Diversion control shifts some portion of the product from food usage to nonfood usage, such as converting potatoes into alcohol. (c) Allocation control is the allocation of supplies from fresh product utilization in a way that will gain more dollars.

There are limitations to the price farmers may seek through marketing. A higher price means that a smaller quantity will be taken from the market informally. Less will be needed since less will be purchased by consumers at these higher prices. If prices are too high, other suppliers may offer consumers some new substitute for the product, perhaps even synthetics, thus permanently reducing the demand for the product.

Marketing Efficiencies

Gains may be obtained by developing a more efficient marketing system through improved production and marketing practices. Gains come through mutual cooperation among parties seeking benefits. Gains may come by increasing efficiency of present activities or by integrating steps within the marketing system. Increased use of bargaining power to improve farm prices and income is being attempted by various producer organizations over the country. Higher prices and better terms of sale have been negotiated. Some gains in returns have been realized through market coordination and other efficiencies.

A good marketing association that has the ability and desire can assist the bargaining association in the handling of multiple products. This offers possibilities for diversion from one market use to another in order to exert the economic pressure through an adjustment of supply.

Farmers in their marketing organizations can use nonprice competitive techniques to build a bigger market at home or abroad. These nonprice techniques would include advertising, merchandising of new and improved products, new packaging, and other services which enhance consumer purchases.

The more substitutes there are, the easier it is for the consumers to substitute and the more difficult becomes the bargaining process. The practical limit to price increases in farm products depends mainly on the potential number of substitutes for the product, the quality of the substitutes, and the market growth for the product.

And Now, How to Act?

Economic considerations lie at the root of farmers' efforts to organize for collective bargaining. To the extent that these economic realities are heeded, farmers can be successful in their efforts. To the extent that these considerations are neglected, farmers will fail in their quest for bargaining power to set the prices for their products.

The ideas presented in this analysis should help the Christian in his task of judging between the wise and the unwise, the effective and the ineffective, the realistic and the unrealistic approaches to collective bargaining for farmers. The Christian's duty, then, is to act as he understands the facts, in light of his discussions with his brothers and the guidance of the spirit of the living Christ.

F. INTERNATIONAL DEVELOPMENT

International Aid and Development

President Fredrik A. Schiotz in his report to the 1968 Convention drew attention to the acute problems of hunger and the urgency of measures to expedite international aid and development. In response the 1968 Convention adopted the following resolution.

WHEREAS, The report of the president to this General Convention has drawn attention both to the great needs of the developing nations and to the relation of possible reduction in armaments to effective social reconstruction; and

WHEREAS, This convention has approved a position paper on "Hunger in the World" which emphasizes the complexity and interrelatedness of the problems; therefore be it

Resolved, That The American Lutheran Church urge reevaluation of the objectives, priorities, and programs of American public policy intended to provide aid to the developing nations of the world; and be it further

Resolved, That The American Lutheran Church acknowledge the necessity of a greater contribution by the United States to assist the developing nations of the world, especially through multilateral approaches to capital investment; and be it further

Resolved, That the next president of the United States be encouraged to include in his foreign policy a challenge to the Soviet Union to a planned, mutual, verifiable reduction in armaments so that the saving of funds thus effected can be applied to social reconstruction at home and abroad; and be it further

Resolved, That The American Lutheran Church express its belief that the proposal of the Uppsala Assembly of the World Council of Churches, concerning a one percent tax on the Gross National Product to be allocated for development purposes in the emerging nations, merits careful consideration, along with other measures intended to accomplish the same purpose.

Hunger in the World

The following statement, prepared by the Commission on Research and Social Action, was adopted by the 1968 Convention "as a position paper," on recommendation of the Joint Council.

The American Lutheran Church notes with strong approval the widespread concern for the tragic dimensions of hunger and poverty, not only in the United States but throughout the world. For, famine indeed stalks the earth. Hunger and malnutrition kill millions of persons and stunt or cripple the development of other millions each year. The grim prospect is that the massive problem of hunger in the world will grow worse before effective countermeasures can be realized.

As men become more sensitively informed about the problem of hunger in the world, there is greater hope for corrective action. Christian love and compassion indeed compel us to press a constructive, coordinated, attack on problems associated with hunger. As we pray our Lord's petition, "Give us this day our daily bread" we include all men everywhere in our thoughts. With Dr. Martin Luther we understand "daily bread" to mean:

Everything required to satisfy our bodily needs, such as food and clothing, house and home, fields and flocks, money and property; a pious spouse and good children, trustworthy servants, godly and pious rulers, good government, seasonable weather, peace and health, order and honor; true friends, faithful neighbors, and the like. (Tappert, *The Book of Concord,* page 347.)

The alleviation of the problem of hunger in the world clearly calls for more than an improved agriculture. It requires the participation of every social institution and every structure of society. It involves family, education, health, housing, religion, science and technology, transportation and communication, commerce and industry, and a government both responsive and effective. Hunger and malnutrition result from such factors as denial of opportunities, economic inequities, social injustice, flood or drought or other natural disasters, wars and the armaments race, population growth occasioned by a marked excess of births over deaths, an imbalance between population numbers and maximum use of available natural resources, a shortage of investment and development capital, escapist outlooks on life which fail to exercise man's dominion over the earth, a lack of personal discipline or application of human energies, and the sheer accumulated weight of unsolved social, economic, political, and technological problems.

The relief of hunger in the younger nations especially is associated with socioeconomic attitudes, values, and programs. Forms and varieties of incentives need to be expanded to stimulate men willingly to engage in economic activities essential to a healthy, balanced, national development. Prestige and respect must be given those producing food for markets. The comparatively scarce capital resources must be allocated to projects of basic economic urgency, not to enterprises of dubious productive usefulness. Comprehensive systems of social insurance are required for the care of the infirmed, aged, handicapped, and dependent. Superior education, power, or prestige must be regarded as resources to be turned to community betterment rather than as signs of progress on the social ladder. Nature and the processes of nature need to be viewed not with superstition or fear but as an endowment over which man must exercise management skills.

As a people made comparatively wealthy through their management of the resources abundantly entrusted to them, Americans have a special obligation in this era of world hunger. We should turn our enormous agricultural productivity in larger measure to supply emergency food aid. We should release more of our scientists and technologists to work with those of the younger nations in the slow task of adapting and developing food production, processing, and distribution techniques suitable to specific climates and cultures. We should provide more funds in loans or in grants for development of basic public services and facilities. We should encourage governments to foster policies in which private skills and investment enterprises can play their wholesome role in the economic development of the country. We should assist in the orderly redevelopment of the complex system of interrelated social institutions and social structures needed to achieve the goals and foster the values each country seeks for itself. We should assist not only with health and nutrition measures but also with disseminating information for effective, but voluntary, reproduction controls. We should enlarge our support of and participation in the various international agencies which approach their tasks on a multi-lateral rather than a bi-lateral basis. We should see the people of other nations as persons with typical human aspirations.

As Christians we are deeply aware of God's grace as well as of man's sin. We see that God causes his sun to shine and his rain to fall alike on the just and the unjust. We believe that he wishes all men to have and to enjoy their "daily bread." We understand that it displeases him when corrupt or malfunctioning social institutions oppress and exploit men and deny them a just measure of the daily bread that should be theirs. We know, too, that the covetous heart of man is ever-active. The comfortable one wishes to keep for himself all those goods and resources he presently enjoys. The disadvantaged wishes for himself that which he sees another enjoying. Yet man also is capable of enlightened self-interest. He can be cooperative, ready and willing to yield his narrow interests in support of larger, mutually helpful goals.

We commend our governmental officials and the leaders of voluntary agencies in their constructive attacks on the problem of hunger in the world. We encourage their resourceful explorations which seek more effective ways of meeting this human problem. We appreciate the difficulties they encounter as they grapple with the complex involvement of a problem which some people feel could be solved simply by turning American agriculture loose to feed the world. We rejoice over cooperative efforts of governmental and voluntary agencies in the slow and tedious tasks of an economic and social redevelopment that respects the cultural expectations and climatic realities of each nation. We endorse measures to provide reliable family planning information to all who wish to use it. We are confident that this measure will alleviate the hunger problem and also may raise the valuation placed upon children and upon human life in general. We know that food, agricultural technology, and patient scientific research and development are weapons to be used with calculated effect to advance not so much our nation's self-interest as the health and strength of the whole family of mankind.

We call upon members of The American Lutheran Church to promote and to support constructively helpful efforts of both governmental and voluntary agencies to solve the world hunger problem. Our faith moves us to help people regardless of lines of race, nationality, or religious persuasion. We are to do good to all men, to bear one another's burdens, even to feed our enemies. We cannot allow pride, arrogance, assumptions of superiority, or nationalistic aspirations to block pathways to wise and informed action. We know that as we help people in such specific crises as hunger, thirst, or loneliness, we serve our Lord himself. (See Matt. 25:31-46.)

In all that we have said, in order to prick the conscience of the comfortable into action to help the hungry, we are deeply aware of the complexities of the problem. We know that man does not live by bread alone, yet he needs bread to live. We know the danger of substituting a new economic colonialism for a former political dependency. We know that in improving health and medical care we intensify population pressures. We know that technology can be destructive of human values. We know how difficult it is to help people without making them dependent or destroying their own integrity. We know that the demands for national freedom and independence represent demands for acceptance of national heritage and aspirations in free parity with others. We know that individual accountability and social accountability, individual freedom and social responsibility, operate constantly in tension. Yet, recognizing the problems involved we still dare to pray, for all men, "Give us this day our daily bread."

G. TAX REFORM

The following statement on "Tax Reform: A Cause for Christian Action" builds in part on portions of the 1964 and 1966 approved statement on "Church State Relations in the U.S.A." Prepared by the Commission on Research and Social Action in 1969 it was recommended by the 1970 Church Council for Convention adoption. The Convention approved it as "a statement of issues for the general information of the members of The American Lutheran Church and as an aid to the discussions seeking an informed solution to a difficult problem of contemporary life and society."

Taxes inescapably, by obligation and by desire, are a concern of the Christian. Paying taxes is listed in the Bible as a Christian's duty toward his government. A good government must be just and must foster conditions assuring the well-being of all the people subject to its rule. Taxes are a means to this end. They determine who shall bear, and who shall be excused from bearing, the costs of government. Taxes provide an impersonal means for channeling the obligations of neighbor to neighbor. Tax policies give opportunity for the strong to exploit the weak, or for the poor to exploit the rich. Tax policies reflect decisions as to where priorities ought to be placed. They shape the manner and the direction in which public resources will be used.

The inequalities, inequities, and injustices which America's systems of taxation impose cry out for correction. If we who are Christians ignore the situation, we are like the priest and Levite who passed by on the other side of the road. If we are quiet when wrong is done to the poor, the weak, the lowly, or even to our enemy, we desert our Lord's cause. The cry of Psalm 82, "How long will you judge unjustly and show partiality . . ." hits us, as does its charge to "rescue the weak and the needy." Taxes can be an avenue of partiality, unjust and harsh, or an avenue for assisting and relieving distress.

Among the many values our systems of taxation need to safeguard is that of the freedom of voluntary enterprise responsibly to fulfill socially acceptable goals. Tax policies need to keep the economy strong, viable, socially responsible, and capable of accomplishing constructive purposes which contribute to the health of the entire community. Taxes ought never so impoverish either the strong or the weak that they thwart incentive or deny opportunity to do needful things outside the structures of government. Neither ought tax policies place the innocent or the ill-informed but erring taxpayer under the threatening duress of some modern publican. Every taxpayer should be protected in his right to challenge the taxing authorities, and if vindicated to have the costs of the case borne by the agency which erred against him.

We agree that a good tax structure should be simple, workable, and equitable. It should be one in which the public has confidence (a) that it is just, (b) that all persons share in relation to their wealth and resources, (c) that provision is made to excuse from or to reduce taxes to persons in disadvantaged or burdensome situations, and (d) that it fosters and advances sound social goals for which there is strong public support. It should not be so confiscatory that it removes incentives or denies all opportunity for risk-taking or other discretionary uses of the taxpayer's resources.

A tax on income, progressive in ratio to a reasonable maximum but with provision for reduction because of unusual or disadvantaging circumstances, appears to be the necessary core of any modern tax system. General sales taxes, unless exemptions are built into the tax provisions, weigh unduly heavy upon the poor, since virtually all of their income is spent in consumer channels. Excise taxes can be levied selectively, and thus can be either proportional to the use of the taxed item or reflective of presumed ability to pay. The general property tax on real estate is inflexible and overworked, and on personal property or intangibles is difficult to enforce. Nevertheless, some sort of equitable balance among these major forms of taxation appears to be a political necessity. Also necessary is some system for sharing the more efficiently obtained and more equitably derived revenues of larger units of government with smaller units, especially those whose financial resources are limited. Tax reform in the interests of justice, equity, and effectiveness is as essential at the state and local levels as at the federal level of government.

Tax loopholes—unintended openings for tax avoidance, or intended openings to encourage activities which have outlived their usefulness—need to be closed. Loopholes generally serve to transfer a portion of the tax load from the strong and powerful to the weak and defenseless. As such, a loophole is unjust and inequitable. We see possible loopholes in the areas of capital gains, tax-free investments in state and local bonds, unlimited charitable deductions, housing allowance for clergy, depletion and depreciation allowances, hobby-farming, the freedoms of the foundations, and nonrelated business activities conducted by various voluntary not-for-profit organizations, to identify but a few areas requiring scrutiny and possible corrective action. We trust that the corrective action will be sensitive and precise, using a surgical knife and thread rather than a meat axe and rope.

The tax status of churches and of religious organizations inevitably is a question which enters any discussion of tax loopholes. The delicate issue of church-state relations, in relation to the constitutionally safeguarded freedom of religion, is at stake. Nevertheless, as a general observation we believe that churches and religious organizations should receive no more, and no less, favored tax treatment than do voluntary associations organized and operated for charitable, scientific, literary, or educational purposes. As an integral portion of America's pattern of voluntary organizations formed for constructive social purposes, organized religion shares with its kindred not-for-profit neighbors the need for government's benign encouragement.

We agree that churches owning real properties and conducting businesses not exclusively and solely essential to their religious, charitable, or educational ministry ought to be subject to tax laws and policies equally applicable to those governing profit-seeking individuals, partnerships, and corporations. We suggest that churches should expect to bear equitable taxation upon their parsonages and other dwelling or residential units in which their staff members reside. We hold firmly to the position that tax exemption of church buildings owned and used directly and solely for worship, educational, and charitable purposes is a sound exercise of public policy. Churches should expect to pay service charges to the municipality for specific services provided the church.

Taxes are too important an issue to be left solely to legislators and administrators. Tax policies deserve the attention of the public in general and of Christians in particular. Tax systems of course are complex. Yet, taxes are tools of social control, to raise and redistribute income and to apply social force. Key, critical, probing questions need to be raised about their goals and the means for reaching those goals. What does a particular tax—or tax exemption—do to the total structure of society? Is a particular tax, or exemption from tax, the best way to achieve the agreed-upon purposes? Where, and how far, do we want our social policies and purposes to move us? What are the underlying motives and rationale for supporting or for opposing a particular tax or tax exemption? Who is ready to speak for tax reform when he presently enjoys preferential benefits? Will the ease of obtaining taxes contribute to governmental overexpansion and perpetuate governmental inefficiencies?

Answers to these questions we cannot give as a corporate church. By raising them we indicate our conviction that taxes are a Christian concern, far broader than merely economic issue. We express our desire that Christians join vigorously in the discussions seeking tax reform. We believe that in the interests of justice and equity, of opportunity and of responsibility, tax reform indeed is a cause for Christian action. As we understand it, the obligation to pay taxes (see for example Romans 13:6-7 or Luke 20:22-25) is closely related to the obligation of government to be just, fair, equitable, impartial, and discerning in its decisions of how to use its power to advance whatever is good and to curb whatever is evil. A sound tax policy is advantageous to both church and state.

H. THE CHURCH'S ECONOMIC PRACTICES*

Commercialism in the Church

Prepared under the leadership of the Commission on Research and Social Action, with particular assistance from Stewardship and Church Women, this statement on "Commercialism in the Church" was adopted by the 1964 Convention, via the following resolution:

WHEREAS, Even a slight taint of commercialism in or in the name of the church jeopardizes the good name and integrity of the church; and

WHEREAS, The correction of any possible abuses in this direction can best be done in love by pointing out a better way; therefore be it

Resolved, That The American Lutheran Church commend the statement on commercialism in the church to pastors and congregations, as well as boards, agencies, institutions and auxiliaries of The American Lutheran Church, as a guide to their own policies and action.

By "commercialism in the church" we mean the ownership and management of income-producing properties and businesses and the selling of goods and services in the name of the church, for the purpose of obtaining funds to finance the programs and operations of the church, its congregations, auxiliaries, and institutions.

A charge of commercialism could apply when the church and its institutions take advantage of tax laws by engaging in activities unrelated to their exclusively religious, charitable, or educational purposes. Any deviation in sources of income or in manner and variety of activities from those "operated exclusively for religious purposes" jeopardizes the tax immunity of the church and its institutions and may deprive its members and contributors of the privilege of income tax deductibility for their contributions.

Such commercialism, we believe, interferes with and confuses the true task of the church, it weakens and impoverishes the spiritual life of the church, it exploits church membership for pecuniary advantage, and it damages the nonmembers' picture of the church. We hold that the church, including its congregations, auxiliaries, and institutions, must be a public example of faithful obedience to all rightful laws affecting its operations as a temporal organization.

While we question whether commercialism currently is a serious problem within the ALC, the church faces a constant temptation to turn to commercial and quasi-commercial sources for raising funds to support the mission of the church. This temptation we believe

---

* Refer also to Chapter V, B, Project Equality, p. 113.

should be resisted. Should corrective measures be necessary in specific situations, we urge that they be handled in an evangelical Christian manner. Patient teaching is called for, showing the better way that manifests the fruits of the Spirit according to the measure of grace that has been given (Gal. 5:22, 23; Eph. 2:4-10). This teaching should be done in the spirit of Section "IV. Christian Liberty" of the "United Testimony on Faith and Life," pages 183-185 of the *Handbook of The American Lutheran Church*.

Recognizing the difficulty of determining motives, we believe, nevertheless, that evident motives should be considered in evaluating church activities and offers of contributions from nonmembers. Church-sponsored activities may seek primarily to foster fellowship within the congregation and community or may provide a needed community service which no other agency can provide, the hope of profit or financial gain being incidental to the prime objective. Contributors to certain activities may wish to assist a cause in which they genuinely believe but others of them may be easing a guilty conscience, seeking to blunt church criticism of their activities or lines of business, or taking personal advantage of provisions in tax laws. The church and its institutions must exercise caution that they do not unwittingly facilitate, or even appear to facilitate, evasions of proper tax liability.

Motivated by these convictions, and speaking in the spirit of Christian love and evangelical freedom, we offer the following observations for the thoughtful consideration of congregations and members of the ALC.

a. Means used to raise funds to finance the work of congregations, the institutions of the church, and the world-wide program of the ALC should be scrupulously consistent both with the spiritual character of the church and its status as a religious not-for-profit corporation registered and protected under the laws of the state (Matt. 22:15-22; 28:19, 20).

b. The free, generous, cheerful giving of money, goods, and selfless service are the marks of the Christian stewardship of its members which ought to be amply sufficient to finance the work of the church. This stewardship is motivated by response to God's love, the claims of the Christian fellowship, and the needs of neighbor (2 Cor. 8:3-5; 9:6-15).

c. Growth in the grace of Christian giving and stewardship expression may be hindered when the church and its agencies engage in such commercial practices as the buying and selling of merchandise, the offering of restaurant or catering services, expectation of preferential discounts, speculation in or management of real estate, or operation of business services not essential to the unique ministry of the church (Matt. 6:33; Mark 11:15-17).

d. Particularly repugnant to The American Lutheran Church are such fund-raising methods as lotteries, games of chance, and any others bearing even a taint of gambling, which frequently is forbidden by state law and always is an offense to the sensitive Christian conscience (Ex. 20:17; Rom. 13:9).

e. Wholesome Christian fellowship which builds bonds of unity and devotion both among the members of the congregation and for the cause of Jesus Christ is a basic and important objective for the church and ought not be confused or bound up with efforts that have money-raising as their dominant goal (Ps. 133; Isa. 55:1, 2; John 15:12-17).

f. The congregation should neither seek nor expect from those outside the church their direct gifts, support, purchases, patronage, or preferential pricing in support of the ministry of Jesus Christ to which the church is committed (Luke 10:2-11). Where men outside the church are moved to assist in the church's program, such help should be gratefully received, provided its acceptance creates no problem of conscience for the church.

g. Danger inheres for the church and its institutions when they build programs or facilities which place major reliance for their development and maintenance upon financial support derived from monmembers, however welcome or beneficial these contributions may be (Luke 14:28-30).

h. The fact that organizations, associations, or activities which are neither organically related to The American Lutheran Church nor subject to its policies and controls bear the name "Lutheran" in their corporate title ought to give them no privileged status in or corporate support from congregations of The American Lutheran Church, however beneficial or useful their services may be to Lutheran persons (Matt. 7:21-23).

i. Concern for commercialism in the church should not preclude faithful use of resources to advance the church's unique ministry, careful fiscal controls, prudent investment policies, and skilled techniques of administration. These are qualities the members rightfully can expect of their church (Matt. 10:16; Col. 1:9-14).

j. Because of its specific status under corporate law, with the tax benefits thus given, the church is obligated ethically as well as legally to confine its activities to those which fulfill its declared purposes as a church or religious organization, recognizing that only so long as and to the extent that it adheres to these purposes can it claim its beneficial immunities from taxation (Zech. 4:6; Matt. 17:24-27; Acts 1:8).

k. Continued protection by the state of the religious freedoms guaranteed the church and its members will be fostered by rigorous adherence to both the letter and the spirit of the charter or articles of incorporation by which units of the church were granted legal status as a religious, charitable, or educational, not-for-profit, corporation (1 Thess. 5:12-22).

l. The American Lutheran Church itself, and each congregation and institution of the ALC, periodically ought to review its entire program, including the ownership and management of any properties and investments it may have and the fund-raising projects of each of its auxiliaries, to determine how well it practices the concepts of Christian stewardship and avoids the temptation to derive revenues from commercial or quasi-commercial activities (1 Peter 3:8-17).

Credit Unions

One of the first assignments made to the Commission on Research and Social Action, on the basis of a request from one of the uniting church bodies, was the development of a "Position Statement on Credit Unions." This statement was approved by the Church Council in 1961 "as a position statement for referral to congregations, institutions, and agencies of the church."

A credit union is a cooperative association of share-holding members who pool their savings and aid one another with low-cost loans. Affairs are managed by a board of directors elected by and responsible to the members.

Membership is restricted to a defined, natural, and cohesive group, usually relatively small in numbers. The emphasis is upon personal relations, character and integrity, loyalty to fellow-members, mutual confidence and trust, and helpfulness in time of need.

As presently operating, the credit union movement serves especially lower-income persons who have sound needs for credit but who can obtain credit only at unduly high costs. It safeguards its clients from unwise uses of credit and from unscrupulous money-lenders.

Credit unions are chartered and supervised by both federal and state governments. They are banded together in state leagues and in the Credit Union National Association, Inc., Madison 1, Wisconsin. Their success appears to depend on the interest and enthusiasm of the members, the judgment of the volunteer boards and committees that manage their affairs, the consistency with which the members deposit savings, and the unity and cohesiveness of the group eligible for membership.

Roman Catholic encouragement of the Credit Union movement has been clear and consistent. Numerous Protestant-related groups also have established credit unions.

For congregations, conferences, institutions, and agencies of The American Lutheran Church to sponsor credit unions for their members or employees is an action thoroughly consistent with their Christian allegiance. If they decide, however, to sponsor a credit union they must zealously guard that it meet and maintain highest standards of performance, genuinely serve the otherwise unmet needs of the members, and remain a unifying factor in the life of the organization to which the credit union is related.

Church Edifices

The Luther League in its Report to the 1968 Convention recommended "that the church convention establish a moratorium on all building within the ALC and its congregations and that it urge strict adherence to such a moratorium by all congregations and institutions of the ALC." In response the 1968 Convention adopted the following resolution:

"To receive with appreciation the Board of Luther League concern with the edifice complex of the church and urge a redirection of priorities and financial investments of the church to effect its mission particularly in regard to the critical national and world issues that confront us, and to request each delegate to communicate this concern throughout the church."

The Church as Employer

Referrals by the 1966 Convention seeking position statements on employment practices in the church and on equal employment opportunity in the church were consolidated into the statement on "The Church as Employer," prepared by the Commission on Research and Social Action. The 1968 Convention adopted the statement on "The Church as Employer" "as a guide to congregations, institutions and agencies, districts, and boards of The American Lutheran Church in their personnel practices."

Who Are Its Employees?

The church has a unique function, "the ministry of teaching the gospel and administering the sacraments." It has a unique character, being "the assembly of all believers among whom the gospel is preached in its purity and the holy sacraments are administered according to the gospel." (See Augsburg Confession, Articles V and VII.) At the same time the church is a social institution operating in this world, a corporate, not-for-profit, entity, legally established, which is protected by and subject to civil laws and ordinances and to the economic realities of the market place. The church dare never so "spiritualize" its status as to deny the implications of the creation and the incarnation.

Functioning in this world The American Lutheran Church today accepts the necessity for full-time workers to carry out various of its functions. This necessity creates the fact of paid, employed personnel and of paying, employing constituency. The American Lutheran Church takes seriously, as counsel addressed directly to it, the message of 1 Cor. 9:3-14 which declares the right to receive material rewards for sowing spiritual good. The church engages pastors, teachers and professors, nurses and social workers, secretaries and custodians, administrators and many other types of workers to carry out the work of its congregations, institutions and agencies, districts and synod. Having a corps of employed personnel, the church and its various units can and should be expected to be regarded as an employer. Faithful to its Lord, the church should aspire to be an exemplary employer.

Complementing and supplementing the services of full-time staff persons are short-term or part-time workers and persons who give freely, without compensation, of their time and energies to the work of the church. Without the involvement and commitment of countless consecrated volunteers the church, humanly speaking, would be unable to fulfill its mission. It cannot depend solely on its paid staff. The church should never be guilty of exploiting their zeal, good will, or consecration. The interests, dedication, and commitment of these persons need to be guarded and protected by the church which accepts their services.

Mutual Expectations

The church can expect from each of its employees and its volunteers a commitment to its mission, a dedication to its purposes, a loyalty to the Lord, and obedience to his Word and will. The church also can expect of all of its workers competence for their positions, faithfulness in the discharge of their responsibilities, and loyal and creative support for the corporate operating policies of the unit of the church in which they serve.

Employees of the church have a right to expect from their salary-paying organization the protection, benefits, and guarantees the laws of the state assure to all employees and to volunteers in the service of voluntary, not-for-profit organizations. Churches should not be exempt from wages and hours provisions, health and safety standards, workmen's compensation and disability protections, unemployment and retirement coverage, liability protection, or similar laws designed to protect persons in their service.

When conditions so warrant the church should stand ready to engage in good faith in collective bargaining with groups of its employees.

Compensation Problems

As an employer the church encounters the economic facts of a money economy. Ordinarily the church no longer can engage its personnel through gifts-in-kind arrangements or through the denial and self-support system of religious communities. Nor should the church exploit the good will of its employees who by serving at salaries substantially below competitive levels may contribute up to thousands of dollars a year to the church. All members of the church should share according to their ability in the support of the church in order to pay equitable salaries for full-time workers in the employ of the church.

A desirable program for the church operating as an employer in today's economy calls for it to:

(a) establish job classifications and standards of work performance, of evaluation and supervision, and systems of enforcing them that will assure the church a fair return for its salary expenditures;

(b) set salaries for church workers at levels that will be competitive for the level of competence, education, and other qualifications required, paying the prevailing market rates for the kinds of service expected;

(c) recruit employees, in terms of their qualifications, and pay competitively to obtain and retain their services;

(d) determine the size of its employment force, as well as the priority of services to which the church assigns its manpower, by the sum of money the members contribute, divided by the amount of the competitive salaries that must be paid.

Workers in the church, including its volunteers, need opportunity for growth, for renewal and recreation, for participation in institutes and retreats, for the spirit of truth to come into and to guide their lives. The church in its employment practices needs to provide adequately for holidays and vacations, and for promoting professional growth and in-service educational opportunities. The church will be amply repaid in the improved quality of services rendered as a result of these growth experiences.

Selective Hiring Practices

To be most effective the church may occasionally seek out and employ persons of a particular race, language, nationality background, or socio-economic status. These persons are uniquely qualified to perform the functions the church needs at that strategic time and place. In so deciding, however, the church must avoid any semblance of denial of opportunity to persons solely on these criteria, lest it betray its trust or impoverish itself through failure to use the abundance of talent open to it. The church also needs to be sure that if it sets denominational membership requirements for any position these indeed are necessary for the competent performance of the duties demanded of that position.

Freed for the Gospel

This concept of the church as employer will benefit the church by enabling it to obtain better qualified personnel, demand higher standards of performance, do justly by its employees, enhance employee morale, and gain self-respect for them and for itself. Thereby the church will increase the value of its own ministry and service alike to the members of the church and to the world.